S0-EKA-440

TIME ENOUGH

Essays in Autobiography

TIME ENOUGH

Essays in Autobiography

By

FRANK LUTHER MOTT

Chapel Hill

THE UNIVERSITY OF NORTH CAROLINA PRESS

WITHDRAWN
Pierce Library
Eastern Oregon University
From1410 U Library
La Grande, OR 97850

Copyright © 1962 by

The University of North Carolina Press

Manufactured in the United States of America

PRINTED BY THE SEEMAN PRINTERY, DURHAM, N. C.

To
Vera

Contents

TIME ENOUGH

Essays in Autobiography

1

Quaker Boy

THOSE BENCHES WERE HARD, especially for a small boy who must sit on them quietly throughout two hours of silent Meeting. Was it really two hours? I cannot be sure. Perhaps as the watch in my grandfather's pocket ticked, it was only one; but as a boy's impatience grew and his hunger sharpened, it was at least two.

And yet I do not recall any unbearable restlessness. I found Meeting generally pleasant, especially for the first half of it. Here were all these good people—our neighbors—sitting with us quietly, clean in their First Day raiment, clean in their hearts and minds. Each was retired a little into his own cell of contemplation, but all were together in the sight of God and man.

As I look back upon those Friends' Meetings, those assemblies on benches within bare walls, of good people whose spiritual ears were attuned for a while to the still, small voice, they seem to me a grand object lesson in the immanence of God—that doctrine beloved of the New England transcendentalists. Indeed, Ralph Waldo Emerson once told a distant relative of mine (James Mott, husband of Lucretia) that if he could bring himself to subscribe to any established creed it would be that of the Society of Friends. What drew him toward this "peculiar people" was their dependence on the authority of the inner voice, so perfectly and simply exemplified in the congregational waiting on the spirit in Meeting.

My grandmother once gave me a copy of *The Essays of Elia,* which she valued for its piece called "A Quakers' Meeting." "The Abbey Church at Westminster hath nothing so solemn, so spirit-soothing, as the naked walls and benches of a Quakers' Meeting," wrote poor Lamb, whose spirit often needed soothing. "Here are no tombs, no inscriptions," he continued; "but here is something which throws Antiquity herself into the foreground— *Silence*—eldest of things, language of old Night, primitive discourser, to which the insolent decays of moldering grandeur have but arrived by a violent and unnatural progression. How reverend is the view of these hushed heads, looking tranquillity!"

Though these things were not much discussed by the Friends I knew (certainly not in eloquent terms), I believe they were adumbrated in the thinking and feeling of the group and the community. For myself, I felt them easily and lightly, as a boy feels and understands the verities; and they afforded me a kind of mild joy.

Meeting was pleasanter in summer than in winter. In cold weather the iron heating-stoves had to be replenished interestingly and with some noise; but the air was heavier and more somniferous, and Meeting seemed longer, and there was likelier to be a crying baby in the "women's part." But in summertime, the meetinghouse was a part of the quiet country scene. Through the open windows drifted familiar rural sounds. There was the stomping of the horses hitched in the sheds nearby— horses patient as boys must be against the time of driving home to First Day dinner. There was the cawing of crows holding their own Meeting in the trees of our meetinghouse grove; but such raucous disrespect of Sabbath calm served only to emphasize the general quiet. There were the occasional liquid notes of a meadowlark; sad voices of the turtledoves, sounding deceptively far-off; the distant bawling of a calf and the barking of a dog; the light hum of bees—those country sounds which were as much a part of the Iowa landscape as the growing corn and the feeding cattle.

Perhaps my thoughts should have been more religious, but the trouble was—and is—that I have never been quite sure just where common life leaves off and religion begins: body and mind and soul seem never to keep decorously each to its own precincts. I know that always on these occasions I was fascinated by the appearance of the elder Friends who sat "facing meeting"; and for hours I would study those wonderful faces, compare them in my mind with portraits of famous men in the books of biography in my father's library, and try over and over to delineate them in words. It was my own private game.

For those who have never had the experience of attending an old-fashioned Friends' Meeting, I must explain what the meetinghouse was like and how the people were seated. I shall describe here the Hickory Grove Meetinghouse, near Yankee Corners, east of West Branch, Iowa, as it stood in the 1890's. It was later "improved" somewhat, by the addition of thin cushions for those hard benches and roofs over all three of the porches. But the building I tell you about here conformed nearly enough to the houses of worship used for many years in England and America by the "Society of Friends, commonly called Quakers"—to use the phrase often employed by Quaker writers themselves.

The Hickory Grove Meetinghouse was in the country, and it suited the country landscape of fields and farms, modest homes, groves and streams, and dirt roads. It was a plain, white, one-story structure without steeple or stained glass. There was a porch on three sides of it, roofed over on the "women's part," to afford seemly ingress and egress, for there were no lobbies nor foyers nor corridors inside, but only the plain meeting-room of the congregation. This room was divided down the center by a partition (invariably pronounced "petition") which separated the benches for the women from those for the men. During First Day and Fourth Day Meetings, this partition was rolled down so that it stood only as high as the backs of the benches; but at Preparative Meeting and at the Seventh Day business sessions held in connection with Quarterly Meeting, it was raised, and the men and women met separately. But even when the shutters were down so that men and women might worship together, the "petition" was an effective barrier of attention, for the eyes of the worshipers, when not lowered, were always straight ahead. Always? Well, almost always. Young men's glances sometimes sought out pretty faces beneath the short bonnets which the younger women wore, despite partitions; but however conscious the girls were of such inspection, answering smiles would have been "unbecoming," and feminine eyes were strictly controlled, if mounting blushes were not.

There was no pulpit in this church, for regular preaching was precluded by Friends' testimony against "the hireling clergy." Nor was there any organ, for Friends classed music with dancing as an incitement to vanity and lust, and a lure that might turn one's steps toward a path infested with strange will-o'-the-wisps of evil and bordered by bright flowers of sin. No; within this meetinghouse, all was bare simplicity, suited to the contemplative silence which was the badge of its character.

There was an aisle down the middle of the "men's

part," and a similar one in the "women's part," and also a space between the benches where most of the congregation sat and the "facing seats." Three "facing benches" looked toward the rest of the Meeting—as a preacher faces his congregation—and each one was raised a step higher than the one before. Thus the highest "facing seats" looked out over the little gathering from a slight point of vantage and honor: here sat the eldest and most respected men of the Meeting. And on the highest "facing bench" and in the seat next to the partition sat the Friend who officiated as "head of Meeting."

My grandfather was head of Hickory Grove Meeting for many years. He was a kindly, patient man, a mystic (as all Quakers must be mystics), and the most simple-hearted man I have ever known. What I mean is that, in spite of the many troubles and serious misfortunes that he encountered, his feeling of the nearness of God was so powerful that there were few complications and no real problems in his own life: he could accept all that came with equanimity. For me, he expressed then and now the essence of Quakerism, which is an inner glow of divinity, quite without pride and with perfect simplicity.

Those old men who sat in the "facing seats" had a fascination for me that I still feel. The names I have forgotten, or remember but vaguely. Neighbor Joseph Armstrong was big and burly and had a florid face and liquid brown eyes. Daniel Pierce was a tall, gaunt man with lined forehead and furrowed cheeks and bristling white hair. I wish I could remember the name of the good Friend, short and roly-poly, who always kept his eyes closed during Meeting. Grandmother assured me he did not sleep, but was merely resting his eyes; certainly he never snored, nor did his head bobble. Isaac Thomas always kept his hat on throughout the meeting; it was a high-crowned, brown straw hat which Isaac pulled down until the brim rested on his ears and eyebrows. Several of the men wore their hats all through the service. Others came into Meeting and seated themselves hatted; then, if it was more comfortable on a hot day, having made their testimony, they laid their hats aside. This was all a vestige of that bold gesture by which George Fox testified to his consciousness of the God-within-him by wearing his hat before king and bishops. But, hatted or hatless, these old men arrested attention by the marks their features bore of strength and weakness, of patience and calm. They were faces weathered by toil and life and sometimes by thought and suffering.

Grandfather's face was singularly unlined and serene, and his clear grey eyes bespoke a soul at peace with man and God. I heard him preach only once, and then he spoke simply and in a mystical tone: it seemed to me he was chiefly quoting Scripture. Joseph Armstrong spoke in Meeting much oftener, and he was wont to fall into the singsong which distinguished much Quaker preaching and which was a result of yielding fully to strong emotions during utterance. Whatever the custom among primitive Friends may have been, I think that at Hickory Grove in the nineties there was some quiet disapproval of the high, cadenced type of address as being overwrought and unseemly. I remember Grandmother's remarking over the stewed chicken of a First Day dinner that "Joseph got to going pretty high this morning." Grandfather made no reply; somehow I sensed his mild disapproval of Joseph's performance and of his wife's comment as well.

But most of the Quaker preaching I remember was inclined rather to monotone than extravagance. There was not much hell-fire and brimstone in it, though there were some rather vague threats of that Outer Darkness into which sinners shall be cast. There was much Paulist exhortation, and the admonition to keep ever in mind "the mark of the high calling" still seems to me more typical than anything else of the preaching I heard in the old Hickory Grove Meetinghouse.

Once in a while some Friend was moved to lift his voice in prayer; he then knelt on the bare floor, while the congregation stood and the men all removed their hats. But it happened many times that nobody was moved to speak at all during Meeting or to pray aloud, and we would have some two hours of what Rufus Jones once called "the corporate hush and stillness of silent meeting."

The last half hour was the hardest for the small boy, especially since he did not know whether it really was a half hour, or an hour, or five minutes. There was no clock, nobody looked at a watch, no bell rang. It was Grandfather's official duty to "break Meeting." That, like the preaching, depended, theoretically, on the movement of the Spirit; but I always suspected that the movement of Grandfather's stomach had something to do with it. I think he never failed to "break Meeting" promptly at twelve o'clock. This was done by the little ceremony of turning to the Friend who sat next him on the top "facing bench" and shaking hands with him; then that Friend turned to the one next him and offered his hand, and soon everyone was shaking hands throughout the Meeting, and rising, and moving slowly outward toward the porches, talking and visiting.

Outside there was a weekly reunion of neighbors—an exchange of greetings and of news about relatives and acquaintances. If the weather was inclement, the visiting had to be done mostly within the meetinghouse; but in the fine weather of summer and fall everyone lingered on the porches for half an hour or more and "spoke with" everyone else. This was before telephones came to the country districts, and neighbors a mile apart would often exchange words with each other only at First Day Meeting. And there was another factor that added interest to this visiting. Since Friends were not permitted to marry outside the Society, the family inter-relations between them all had become many and complicated, and the health of second or third cousins (who had perhaps moved to California or Philadelphia) and the activities of the whole closely integrated group were matters of strong interest to all. It seems to me that health and crops and babies were the main topics of this babble of conversation.

"And how is thy rheumatism now, William?"

"Oh, it's still pretty miserable. How are thee and Liddy?"

"I've been well as common, William, but Liddy is still pretty poorly."

Or it might go like this:

"What do you hear from Ellwood and his family?"

"Oh, we had some fine news from them, Amos. They have a new son, born on the third day of Seventh Month—and Hannah and the child are doing well!"

"Well, I do declare! This is their third, isn't it? And all boys?"

"Yes. They did hope for a girl this time, but the boy is healthy—weighed nine pounds and ten ounces!"

And always there were many conversations like this:

"Now, Ruth, we are expecting thee and Richard to dinner today. It won't be much, but——"

"Oh, Abbie, thee oughtn't to do it! I do hope thee won't go to any trouble——"

First Day dinners were wonderful. The cooking was all done on Seventh Day, leaving only the minimum

of warming and table setting and coffee making for
First Day. What baking and cooking and "redding up"
on Seventh Day! Enough to tire out the womenfolk.
But as a result, things were all ready on First Day morning and there was a proper calm before Meeting.

The only excitement on First Day morning came from
dressing in one's best—including Grandfather's putting
on a boiled shirt and his First Day suit and Grandmother's arraying herself in her First Day bonnet. Grandmother had three of those long bonnets—a black one not
quite so long for visits to town and for Fourth Day Meeting, a longer brown-silk one for First Day, and finally one
that I was allowed to see only two or three times—her
Yearly Meeting bonnet, a beautiful long grey-silk one,
made especially for her in Philadelphia and kept in tissue
paper in the lowest drawer of the secretary against the
time when Grandfather and Grandmother made their
biennial pilgrimage to Ohio Yearly Meeting. Also, of
course, there were the smaller calico bonnets for home
wear.

But the First Day bonnet seemed to me very fine.
And it was exciting to climb into the buggy behind old
Nell and set off for Meeting, though Hickory Grove was
less than two miles away. The buggy was high and
difficult for Grandmother to enter. There was a small iron
step on the outside, which was all right for men; but
Grandfather always drove round to the "uppen-block" to
make it easier for Grandmother to get in and for the
three of us to settle into the high, narrow vehicle. Of
course, those "single buggies" were designed for no more
than two occupants, and even a small boy (if he were a
little too big now to sit on his grandmother's lap) could
barely crowd in. So Grandmother had neatly covered a
yeast-box with some remnants of old woolen clothes; and,

placed on the floor just back of the dashboard and between my grandparents' legs, it was a satisfactory seat for me in the buggy, while indoors it served as a footstool. If Nell, in flytime, switched her tail in my face (and a horse's tail is a very keen lash), I bore it with fortitude broken only by childish remonstrances directed against the heedless mare. Nell and Bell were Grandfather's two farm workhorses. I was discouraged from calling Nell "Nellie," because of the temptation to apply a similar diminutive to her teammate—an impropriety to be avoided. Nell, a better driver, was always chosen for the single buggy. Her only fault was a terror of "thrashing engines"; in the fall, when threshing outfits were moving from farm to farm, propelled by their puffy little steam engines, it was not safe to have Nell on the road of a weekday. On First Days, however, Nell shared in the general serenity of the countryside and would negotiate the distance to Meeting just about as fast as a man would walk it. Grandfather never urged her: we started in plenty of time, and we knew Nell had had a hard week's work on the farm.

Coming home after Meeting, it was another story; then Nell "smelled her oats" and was a far livelier nag. Hunger had sharpened all of our appetites, and we were looking forward happily to dinner. Living close to Meeting, we usually brought home as guests some Friends who lived farther away—and perhaps some close neighbors as well. Fowl from our barnyard, meat canned last winter at butchering, vegetables out of our garden in season, fruit from our orchard and berry patches, and Grandmother's famous pies and cakes—better than Lucullan were these homely banquets. Grandmother served two pieces of pie to each diner—apple and custard, for example. This, of course, was in addition to the fruit and cake. We did ourselves well.

After dinner we all gathered in the parlor for visiting. I was never much interested in this talk of my elders, since it was again mostly about relatives, many of whom I had never seen. Often such discussions ran into knotty genealogical problems:

"Thee remembers thy third cousin Obadiah Scott, don't thee, Jonathan?"

"Oh, yes, the one that moved out to Salina, Kansas."

"That's the one. Well, his second wife was a niece of Mary's stepfather—thee knows—John Young." Mary was the speaker's own wife. He now gets to the point: "Well, I was wondering what had become of their oldest girl. She would be a second cousin once removed of our children, and we ought to keep track of her."

"Seems to me I heard she married a Worthington—I think a son of Daniel Pierce's cousin—Samuel, is it?—Samuel Worthington?"

And so on and on, until all became rather sleepy after the heavy meal, and the women adjourned to dish-washing and the men to look over Grandfather's pigs and crops. And the boy stole away to a favorite hide-out in the orchard, to read and nap and dream through the long, warm First Day afternoon.

On Monthly Meeting days, Friends returned to the meetinghouse in the afternoon to decide on any actions to be taken by the group as a whole. Then, and at the Preparative Meeting preceding Quarterly Meeting, their deliberations were presided over by no chairman and led to no votes. The only official was the Clerk, who "made a minute" of any action agreed upon. All decisions were reached by agreement of all rather than by majorities. Here doubtless was an advantage to the negative of any question, for if no agreement was reached, the matter had to be dropped; yet often this meant only a postponement of the issue while elder Friends "labored with" recalcitrants—so that eventually there was agreement, or what passed for it.

At Preparative Meeting the eight disciplinary queries were propounded, so that if any Friends were behaving unsuitably to their profession, report might duly be made. Thus it was that my own father and mother were reported (when I was a child in arms) under the Sixth Query: "Do Friends maintain a faithful testimony against a hireling ministry?" They had moved from a farm in the Coal Creek community of Quakers to the town of What Cheer, where Father had bought a newspaper; and there they had begun attending the Methodist church. The minister of that church doubtless received an inadequate salary, after the custom of the times; but he was beyond doubt a "hireling." There ensued a time of worry and heartbreak, while Friends "labored with" my parents. It was a bitter separation, for Grandfather especially; but Father felt strongly that the testimony of Wilbur Friends with regard to cultural matters and amusements, and their peculiar customs, were a straitening influence which he and his family must abandon. In my boyhood I heard much talk that went back to these anxious and soul-searching times. At length, however, my grandparents had to yield, and David Charles and Mary E. Mott were disowned. ("Diz-zoned" was the word in my childhood, and it meant something very special that "disowned" can never mean.)

My brother and I, as too young to understand, were not "disowned," however; and as far as I know our "birthright" in the Society of Friends was never canceled, despite our sampling of other faiths. I think that as long as

Grandfather lived, both he and Grandmother kept the hope that we boys might come back into the fold. What I have written here about old Quaker life and customs comes mainly from my recollections of long visits to my grandparents' home near West Branch, and later to Grandmother's at Whittier, Iowa.

The narrowing influences of the Wilbur Friends of which my father complained were, first, their testimony against music; second, their intolerance of most art and contemporary literature; and third, a general restriction of association to Friendly circles.

As far as music and the fine arts were concerned, both Father and Mother were too deeply rooted in the old Quakerism ever to find their way even to an appreciation, much less to any practice, in those fields. Some of their children, however, did better; and that was doubtless what had been in their minds.

But in literature the breaking of the old bonds was nothing less than emancipation. Father and Mother had first met at the Friends' boarding school at Barnesville, Ohio; and part of their courtship consisted of reading together a single-volume edition of Shakespeare's plays which they had smuggled into the school despite warnings against the licentiousness of stage-plays that stemmed directly from old George Fox himself. Of course, Quaker homes were not without books. Besides the Bible, most of them had the *Friends' Library*, which consisted of several large volumes containing the religious experiences and testimonies of early Quakers: to me they were inexpressibly dull. Grandfather also had *Paradise Lost*, and Grandmother had Whittier's poems. They took the local weekly newspaper, and even, during one presidential campaign, they allowed themselves the unusual indulgence of subscribing for the Chicago *Inter Ocean*, much of which Grandfather read aloud to us. And of course they received the *Friend* paper, from Philadelphia, sometimes called "the square *Friend*" because of the shape of its pages. But now Father and Mother were no longer limited to such meager fare and began to accumulate a small but choice collection of general literature, of which I shall write later.

There was another kind of liberation which my parents experienced when they left the Society of Friends. Friends had a testimony against the worldly vanity of changing fashions, so the men still "shaved clean," as men did in Fox's time; and all still wore raiment of the same cut and style that the common people had worn at that time—and always in conservative greys, browns, and black. Now Father could—and did—raise a luxuriant red beard, and he could—and did—wear a cutaway coat decorated with lapels when he went to work on his newspaper. Mother could wear a spring hat adorned with flowers to church and W.C.T.U. meetings.

And one other thing: we were no longer required to use what Friends called "the plain language." When the Society was founded in England in the mid-seventeenth century, the use of the titles "Mister," "Mistress," and "Miss," and the plural "you" for "thou" or "thee," were all marks of flattery and obsequiousness, tending to set certain classes above others, whereas all were equal in the sight of God. Hence the continuing testimony of Friends against the use of "Mr." and "Mrs.," the singular "you," and so on. Also, since many of the usual names for the days of the week and the months of the year were of heathen origin (as Thursday for Thor, January for Janus), Friends discarded all such pagan practice for mere numbers; Thursday, for example, became Fifth Day and January, First Month.

But speech habits are not as easy to put off as straight-collared coats; and the Motts, newly moved to the town of What Cheer, had some trouble doffing their "thee's." Father explained to my brother and me that we should soon be starting to school, and the other children would think we were queer if we said "thee" instead of "you." So we made a game of it; and if one of us accidentally dropped a "thee," the other pointed a finger at him and shrilled, "Thee——thee——thee——thee!" Thus by dint of much correction and cajolery we learned to conform. But not so Mother. She was willing to say "you" outside the home, but to the day of her death she always addressed members of her family by the more tender and familiar "thee." If she had ever said "you" to me, it would have sounded in my ears like a curse.

"Thou" was almost unknown among midwestern Friends, except in quotations from the Scripture; and when eastern Friends sometimes used it, it seemed an affectation. "Thee" was both nominative and accusative.

And now, as I write these lines in 1961, the Wilbur Friends have almost vanished into complete oblivion. The Hickory Grove Meeting was "laid down" many years ago; the last I knew, a few descendants of the old Wilbur Friends were meeting on First Days with a few descendants of the Conservative Friends (who, in spite of their name, had been less conservative than the Wilburites) in the little meetinghouse in the village of West Branch, using only the "women's part," since there were so few left of even the combined congregation. As Grandfather used to drive us to the Hickory Grove Meeting on those First Days I have been telling about, we would pass Conservative Friends from a few miles farther east driving the other way to their West Branch Meeting. Now those of both sects who are left sit in silence together.

Such unions have occurred in Ohio, too, where the Wilburites were once so strong. Indeed, the latest directory does not separate the two sects and estimates that there are left in the whole of the United States only some two thousand of the combined communion.

Happily, the old dull controversies are lost in the deepening mists of the past; and the Wilburites, the Gurneyites, the Hicksites, the Conservatives, the Progressives, and the rest tend to make common cause for the peace of the world, the relief of economic and social tensions on various fronts, and a satisfying religious life. An active agency in the new integration was the American Friends Service Committee, operating from the city of "Brotherly Love" founded by Quaker William Penn; the modest but highly effective work of this organization, performed mainly in the aftermath of wars to which Friends continue to register their "conscientious objection," has done more than anything else to bring together the dissident groups of the general Quaker persuasion.

I must confess that in later life I have experienced a feeling of loss in the lapse of my relations with Friends and Friendly attitudes, especially since I have grown to believe that the responsibilities and stresses of our complex life call more than ever for occasional retirement into contemplation. And so I find myself now and again laying down a book or periodical, or sitting back in my office chair, to draw the curtains of tranquillity about me for a little time. Not to daydream, not to worry about duties neglected or tasks imperfectly performed, not to pray in any formal sense—but to meditate for a few moments, by an act of will, upon things removed from the immediate maelstrom, such as an unreasoning faith in the eventual value of good works or the calming conviction that, despite threats of bombs, the extremes of some of the existentialists, and all the wildness about us, I can find in myself a private security in dedication to such things as I hold in highest regard. All this is perhaps a vestigial remnant of the Quaker quietism to which I was born.

And I am increasingly unwilling to take refuge in the alibi that I have no time for such periods of reflection, for I have a firm personal philosophy that any man has time enough for what he wants most to do. Is it not possible that the tremendous wave of leisure that is breaking upon us in America today may afford some hours for profound personal thinking, apart from all pressures? Cannot intelligent persons form a pattern of living in which they may include the Friendly concept of occasional hours—or at least moments—of still contemplation, retiring for a little while into "the eldest of things, language of old Night, primitive discourse"?

2

Country Town

THE LITTLE TOWN OF THE Middle West during the 1890's was something different from the quiet village of New England and New York state. Nor was it like the small southern town or the bustling city-to-be of the West. The kind of little town in which I grew up existed mainly to serve the families who lived on the farms round about. These Iowa farmers were a remarkable race. They were horny-handed sons of toil and all that, but they were much more than mere field laborers. They were, as a rule, strong characters. It seems to me that the dominant quality that characterized most of them was a hardy individualism. Being much alone, in the fields, behind the plow, the farmer had a habit of thinking things out for himself. Usually he raised, besides his crops and livestock, a large family—all within a rather stern discipline of hard work, hearty food, the fear of God, and self-reliance.

The country town was integrated in a thousand ways with this rural life and activity. And yet it had an entity of its own, never completely apart from the farm and the farmers, but designed also to serve those who were serving the farmers. This entity comprised three institutions—the church, the school, and the store. You might think the town churches and schools were wholly for townsfolk; but that would be a mistake, for a few farm families always attended services in town, and a number of country boys and girls came into town to high school. But the store was the real mixing-bowl. Though some of them, like the implement stores, found their patronage nearly all among the farmers, and most of them were inclined to cater to the country trade rather more than to that of the town, it was the stores that demonstrated most definitely the social and economic integration with the rural elements that was the essence of the small town.

I tell the story as I saw it. Whoever wishes to read a historical survey treatment of the Midwestern small town may find a thoughtful and entertaining one in *Main Street on the Middle Border,* by my friend Lewis Atherton; but the "survey" I shall set forth here is one obtained through the observations of a wide-eyed boy who lived in three Iowa towns in the 1890's. One of these places claimed a population of over three thousand; the others each had about two thousand and enjoyed the prestige of being county seats.

My story conflicts with some observations recorded by others, especially with the more jaundiced accounts. Mine was a comparatively happy childhood, and in my recollections of it there is little hate-distortion. I have read many studies of the small town by writers of fiction and by sociologists; and some of them have emphasized its ambitious aping of city ways, some its sexual vices, some its rapacity and propensity to "gouge" its farmer patrons. In those allegations there is almost always some truth, for men and women of many characters made up this village society; but my own memories are chiefly of good, well-intentioned people, a "folksy" society, a healthy environment. Again and again my recollections return to the basically rural nature of the small town as

Pierce Library
Eastern Oregon University
1410 L Avenue
La Grande, OR 97850

I knew it, its green look, its fresh outdoor mood. It was countrified. No suburb this: *sub rure* rather than *sub urbe*.

Church for Editor Mott and his family was the local Methodist church. Church life was organized into a full day of activities on Sunday, prayer meeting on Wednesday night, choir practice on Thursday night, weekday afternoon Aid Society and Missionary Society activities for Mother, and a "protracted meeting" throughout two to six weeks in the winter to warm up the religious emotions of the old church members and get some new ones in.

No lying late abed of a Sunday morning! Up bright and early we were, to get our chores done—milking the cow and cleaning the barn, feeding the chickens, emptying the ashes and filling the woodbox and coal-bucket, and so on—all in plenty of time to wash and dress carefully for Sunday school at ten. This weekly "getting ready" included the blacking of shoes for the family, finding a collection penny and a clean handkerchief for each child, and getting us all started together and in good time in a seemly Sunday procession. Mother, of course, had the oversight of all these details, as well as the responsibility of getting the dinner roast on to cook while we were at services; and in addition she had on her mind thoughts for the Sunday school class of young girls which she was about to teach—a duty which she took very seriously. But I am sure that the Sunday-morning parade of husband and wife followed by four spick-and-span children all setting off for Sunday School was the pride and joy of her heart.

At Sunday school we received cards bearing colored pictures of Bible scenes for attendance prizes and papers to bring home for Sunday reading. Of these, the *Class-*

mate, to which some of the *Youth's Companion* writers sometimes contributed, seemed to me far the best; it was for the older scholars. After Sunday school, we were usually allowed to run home and read our papers and await the return of our elders for Sunday dinner. But occasionally there was a campaign to keep the children for preaching service. One preacher named McKee (would I could forget him!) once promised to give a Bible to each child who would attend morning service for a full year and turn in at the end of that time a schedule of the texts the preacher had used in his fifty-two sermons. I not only fulfilled the requirement but also wrote out each text on a fancy card taken from a set of greeting samples in Father's printing office, all bound together in ribbons with Mother's help. This fancy record of my fidgety attendance at many dull sermons was presented through my Sunday school teacher as intermediary; it mildly amused the Reverend Mr. McKee, who never remembered to give me a Bible.

For Sunday dinner we nearly always had a generous roast of beef, put on the fire in an iron kettle before Sunday school and timed to be done about twenty minutes after twelve. In winter the roast was cooked atop the hard-coal burner in the dining room, in summer on the back of the kitchen stove. If the preacher overran the twelve o'clock closing time for morning service, Mother was on pins and needles; she could smell her roast burning five blocks away. Nor was she the only one. Housewives in general despised long-winded preachers; and most ministers, mindful of this feature of domestic economy, advanced upon "Fifthly and Finally" a few minutes before twelve and finished on the dot—or, well, nearly on the dot.

What wonderful Sunday dinners! Luscious roast

beef, with potatoes browned in its juices; and then, when meat and potatoes had been removed, rich brown gravy made after them in the pot! Perhaps the supreme pleasure was one that was passed around among us children, Sunday after Sunday, of swabbing the bottom of the pot with crusts, thus regaling ourselves with the richest of the gravy on homemade bread.

After dinner, there were naps. There were no games on Sunday, except checkers. I cannot explain this exception, but it is true that Father sometimes indulged in this quiet diversion with us on a Sunday afternoon. Of course, the little ones had to be at "Yunra Lig" at three. Junior League was a branch of Epworth League, the Methodist young people's society. I cannot remember any pleasure in the junior affiliate; but Epworth League, which met before church in the evening, was a challenge to me, because by the time I was fourteen or fifteen I was given the responsibility of organizing programs for some of the meetings. This was fun and fitted in with the training I was receiving at about the same time in "rhetoricals" at school.

Evening services were chiefly for the younger members and the popular audience and became important to me only after I began "going with girls" and singing in the choir. The morning choir was composed of performers of some local reputation, but at the evening service there was a choir of young folks. Seeing the girls home from church at night was exciting—especially the ordeal of asking them. Taking a girl *to* church was almost tantamount to announcing an engagement, but taking her home was different. Boys would line up outside the church door as "church let out" and wait until the girls of their choice emerged. Then a boy would step out and mumble, "See you home?" He did not need to speak very plainly, for the girl understood clearly enough what he was up to. If she said "No," the disappointed swain slunk off quickly into the shadows, hoping against hope that not all his friends had seen him "turned down." It seems strange that there were not frequent fights among rivals at the church door, but such occurrences were rare. It was all decorous and according to a fixed social code which permitted no interference with couples who were "going steady" and which recognized fully the girls' privilege to accept or refuse without insistence or annoyance. Choir practice offered similar opportunities, but there the group was smaller. Epworth League "socials" gave many a boy (myself among them) his first opportunities for dating.

Thus church-affiliated activities, though centered upon Sunday, were by no means limited to that day. Midweek prayer meeting was attended by all of the "pillars" and many of the humbler, but faithful, members. I sometimes went with my mother; and though I was, as a rule, rather bored by the proceedings, I found some interest in the eccentricities of the ancient ones who habitually offered testimony or prayer, or both, at these gatherings. There was one patriarchal saint who prayed every week for all the great of the earth—President McKinley, Queen Victoria, Senator Allison, Admiral Dewey, the governor, the mayor, and so on, down to the preacher and "the few here humbly foregathered in this sanctuary." And another old valetudinarian with creaking joints would kneel painfully and begin, "Here, O Lord, on the bendified knees of this sinfullen, fasticaten body——" and so on. Or at least it sounded like that: what he really was speaking to the Lord about was his "sinful and fast-decaying body." Artificial as prayer meeting seemed,

it doubtless brought "spiritual refreshment" to many by
furnishing an opportunity for religious utterance.

The Ladies' Aid Society was an important part of the
church socially and financially. Was the old aisle carpet
worn out? Talk to the Ladies' Aid about it. Was the
parsonage shabby for want of paint? Call on the Ladies'
Aid. The Aid Society socials, fairs, food sales, and dinners were important community events. The Missionary
Societies were active, too, both Home and Foreign; and
there was some competition between them in fund raising
and sponsored events.

The Easter collection was the great goal and occasion of the Women's Foreign Missionary Society. We
children, who did not receive allowances from our parents
until much later, employed many devices to raise our own
contributions; but everyone had to do his part, for competition between Sunday school classes for the largest
joint donation was keen. One year I dug horse-radish
root, grated it, and put it into old bottles with a little
vinegar and water and sold it about the neighborhood.
I made my grater by cutting a piece of tin from an old
baking-powder can and pounding nail-holes through at
close intervals. The grating was hard on hands, and the
horse-radish got into one's nose and eyes; but the neighbors bought the stuff and liked it, and I had the satisfaction of thinking my dimes helped save the souls of some
of the "heathens."

The Home Missionary activity that I remember best
was the Flower mission, for which we collected great
quantities of home-grown flowers to send to hospitals,
charitable homes, penitentiaries, etc. They were sometimes sent a long way off; I think the express companies
co-operated in the work as a contribution to charity. The
nearest beneficiary of our Flower mission was the county

jail, the few inmates of which were undoubtedly surprised to have their cells brightened by sweet peas and
roses. This gesture of a sentimental penology had some
curious effects, not all of them pleasing to the Missionary
Society; but some stories usually drifted vaguely back of
suffering made easier to bear, hard hearts touched, and
lives reformed by the "ministry of flowers."

The greatest church effort of the year, however, was
the revival meeting, which commonly came in the winter.
The stated objects of this series of gatherings were to
save sinners and to revive the fainting religious spirit of
the church itself. Though the regular minister sometimes
delivered the sermons, professional "revivalists" expert
at showing how sinners were hanging by a hair over the
leaping flames of the pit were sometimes invited in.
Their preaching was dramatic and emotional and they
were skillful in developing a community excitement that
came to a climax in the mesmeric frenzy of the final
meetings. I remember with shame that as a boy I was
led to kneel at the altar, shed tears for my rather in-
definitely confessed sins, and then stand up shaking and
dazed to be "counted for Christ." I have to add that
after these many years I cherish a resentment against
the "revivalists" who caught me in their web of mass
hysteria in my childhood: I fancy that my psyche still
bears the ancient scars of an experience so artfully induced.

A little later, as a high-school lad, I went through a
series of meetings led by William A. ("Billy") Sunday.
This was in the years when the great evangelist, newly
recruited from the ranks of professional baseball, was still
visiting the smaller towns; later he was taken over by
more lucrative service in the great cities. In my home
town his meetings had to be a "union effort," in which

the Methodists and the Presbyterians joined. There was
at first much objection to taking in the Presbyterians,
many of whom (it was whispered) played cards and
danced. But the Reverend Mr. Sunday would come to
Audubon, Iowa, only if the churches would join forces
in one big drive on sin, and he had his way. He also
had his way about an auditorium. The Presbyterians had
a smaller membership but a larger church; the Methodists,
in order to meet the seating capacity challenge, erected
a temporary gallery in their church with the intention of
bringing the meetings within a Methodistic aura. But as
soon as Mr. Sunday got into town and took one look at
the gallery monstrosity, he declared it unsightly, unsafe,
and unsuitable, and moved over to the Presbyterian
church. "Billy" Sunday always ran the show; he created
his own aura.

By this time I was inured to the hypnotics of revival-
ism. Oh, I was loyal to "Billy" and his works; I was on his
side, and I sang in his big choir throughout the meetings.
But I could watch him objectively and analyze his techniques and effects. His acrobatic homiletics were a sight
to behold: with one foot on the seat of a chair and the
other on top of the lectern, he would shake both fists in
the faces of his gaping congregation and call them hypocrites and liars. When he prayed, he took it for granted
that the Lord knew baseball slang as well as Scripture,
and he talked to Him familiarly: "You know I'm doing
the best I can for these hypocrites down here in Audubon,
Iowa, Lord. I've preached Your word till I'm hoarse,
I've held meetings day and night, I've shouted and ago-
nized and prayed. I've worn myself out, but the Devil
has a strangle holt on the people of Audubon, I guess.
I've pitched fast strikes right over the plate, Lord—no
curves. If you know of anything else I can do to make

them quit their lying, and going after other men's wives, and sneaking around to the drugstores for their whisky, and cheating their neighbors, why, just you let me know, Lord, and I'll do it! You know I'll do it if it kills me, Lord!"

There was some disillusion in the aftermath of a series of Billy Sunday meetings. I remember the quarreling after the Audubon meeting about whether the Methodists or the Presbyterians would get this or that new convert, and which church would get more than the other. Also, though all, in the closing days of the meeting, had allowed a mass enthusiasm to sweep them into making a whopping big farewell collection as a testimonial for the evangelist, after he was gone, with the money in his pocket, a feeling grew that it was not a very nice thing to have so much cash taken out of town so easily. Then too, there was the inevitable backsliding. Billy Sunday's athletic figure had scarcely disappeared, waving his hat to the crowd from the rear platform of the single passenger car of the "accommodation train" on the branch line, when word got about that the star convert of the whole meeting was on a sensational bender.

What great centers of our social life the churches were! It seems to me that more than half of the social activities of our town radiated from the church. There were the ice-cream "sociables," the lawn parties, the cake sales, the fairs, the big church dinners, the Ladies' Aid bees, the Epworth League parties, the Christmas Eve exercises (with program and tree and gifts for all), the annual church-wide Sunday school picnic, and more, and more. And the church services themselves, were, of course, social events of importance, where we met and visited with friends and the young people began courtships.

Lodge meetings, for some unregenerates, took the place of church services; but for most people church and lodge seemed to supplement each other, and much was made of the religious teachings in the rituals of the "orders." Protestant ministers commonly belonged to the lodges (sometimes to several) and if they did not "go through the chairs," they at least served as chaplains. Many others would belong to two or three such organizations. My father was a good Mason, an Odd Fellow, and a Knight of Pythias. The costumes of the orders, their marching and parades, and their funeral and Memorial Day services were fascinating to a young boy. It was an impressive sight when a lodge in full regalia would attend church in a body, as most of them did annually.

Some social life clustered also around the schools—especially about the high schools. I have very little memory of my first two years of school. I had been enrolled in the First Room of the What Cheer public schools only a few weeks when I marched in what I faintly remember as a tremendous parade down the main street of town to celebrate the quadricentennial of Columbus' discovery of America, a tiny American flag clutched in my hand.

By the time I reached Third Grade, we moved midyear to Tipton, where my father had bought a newspaper, and there I did very badly in school. Every day was agony to me. Worst was mental arithmetic: 2 plus 7 divided by 3 times 9 plus 3 times 10 less 200 divided by 10. Answer? A flurry of hands waving in the air, but never Frank Mott's hand. He had been lost in confusion and woe away back at "times 9 plus 3." One afternoon Father visited our room; and when we were all lined up at the blackboard, showing off for the editor by doing some quick arithmetic, he saw me peeking at what my neighbor was writing down, in a desperate effort to keep up with the class. Father never punished me for that cheating, except by mentioning it that evening at supper. I am sure our parents were worried about the school relations of both their sons; my brother was having even a harder time than I was, and later in the year was demoted one grade. My worst memory of that painful year is of the public punishment of one of the boys in my class, for what offense I do not now know. He was about twice as big as any other boy in our room; and the Professor (as we called the town superintendent of schools) and the janitor tied him up on two chairs on the rostrum and beat him with straps. I had never known any violence at home nor ever seen much brutality on the playground or anywhere else, and this was a truly shocking experience for me. Maybe it taught us young spectators some kind of lesson, as it was doubtless supposed to do: I am sure it did not teach us to love or respect our elders.

The only thing I remember enjoying in the Third Grade was singing the popular swinging hymn tunes of that time. We always had devotional exercises in the morning (as we had on the day of that memorable beating), and we sang with a will, "Work, for the Night is Coming" and "We Are Washed in the Blood of the Lamb." It was a couple of months after the official beating of the boy in the Third Grade that some of the big boys in the high school caught the Professor in a second-floor corridor and threw him downstairs, nearly breaking his neck. A little later he resigned.

I think such abuses were not very common in Iowa schools in the nineties. In this case there was a political clique which was in control of the courthouse, the town government, and the schools. Father and his newspaper were engaged in a bitter contest with this group, and there was a feeling at our house that the Professor was revenging himself against Father when he demoted my brother; but we were instructed never to say anything of the sort outside of the home, and Mother was the only one who ever expressed herself freely on the subject.

Fourth Grade was far better. Teacher was a large, pretty girl with a pink and white complexion, and we all loved her. On the last day of school we gave her a farewell present. We had a committee on collection of funds for this purpose, another on the choice of a gift, and a third on the presentation. We all dug down to find nickels and pennies to make up what we thought was a fine sum, which we turned over to the purchasing committee; and after much deliberation that group bought a box of toilet soap, very lovely and perfumed. I was on the presentation committee; and Mother, who never failed us on such occasions, supplied verses which she taught me to declaim in proffering the gift. I wish I had those "Verses on Presenting a Box of Soap to Our Dear Teacher" to insert here; alas, they perished with the occasion, but in their time and place they were esteemed beautiful.

Fifth Grade was wonderful. I should like to burn a candle here to the memory of Miss Elizabeth Jones, a teacher who had an abiding interest in the development of the untried minds and budding talents of the boys and girls who passed through the Fifth Room. Miss Jones permitted the son of the Methodist preacher (who was a Bryanite) and me (who idolized McKinley) to debate free silver for half an hour at a time many days during the stirring presidential campaign of 1896. She allowed me to handle, and read during school hours, a volume I shall never forget—*The Rime of the Ancient Mariner* with Gustave Doré's illustrations. She encouraged us to stand on the rostrum and tell stories, and even to spin yarns.

There was a small, good-looking, glib boy in our room
who came from a family which had belonged to a traveling actors' troupe and which, for some reason, had settled
in our town; this lad fascinated all of us by his thrilling
narratives of adventure—some of which, I suspect, came
out of the nickel storybooks which most of us were not
allowed to read. In one of his fables he told us how he
had been "stunted" in his infancy so that he would always
be able to play juvenile roles, but there was nothing
"stunted" about his free-flowing imagination.

On Fridays we sometimes had spelling matches, which
were very exciting. I had just begun to learn to set type
and was therefore rather unexpectedly interested in spelling. But the scholar who was head of our room in all
branches, including spelling, was a girl named Jean.
She was tall and slender, and her light-gold hair, un-
braided, flowed down her back in a shining cascade to her
waist. One Friday afternoon, when everyone else had
gone down and Jean and I were exchanging "phthisic"
and "fuchsia," she suddenly went perfectly white and
sank to the floor in a faint. I had never before seen
anyone faint, and was terrified. I guess I was in love with
Jean, in a distant, fearful way. She was an ice-maiden,
daughter of a stockman-banker who had a palatial home
on the edge of town. I think she died young: I cannot
believe that she grew up to become fat and hearty, bearing
five bouncing babies in a happy marriage. I am sure she
died young.

I do not remember much about the Sixth Grade, and I
think I "skipped" the Seventh when we moved to Audubon. In that town's Eighth Room, I found Miss Ella
M. Stearns, a truly great teacher, who, after making many
generations of grade-school pupils her debtors for life,
served for years as county superintendent of schools. She

was a strong but genial character, whose speech betrayed her New England origins. She was equally good at teaching all of our subjects—history, geography, reading, arithmetic, spelling—but I think we all looked forward most to the half-hour of reading from some fascinating and improving book with which she opened every morning's exercises.

In high school, Miss Harriet Bilharz, with a brand-new diploma from Northwestern University, was a brilliant teacher. It was the first time I had ever had a college graduate as a teacher; and this was an inspiration, for our parents had assured their four children from infancy that they were to have college educations. Under Miss Bilharz I read my first Latin—Caesar's *Commentaries* and the *Aeneid*. But it was under Miss Jennie Riggs, who came a little later, that I devoured every line of every page of Pancoast's *History of English Literature*. As I look this book over now, I find it a singularly dull text; whether it was Miss Riggs who made it exciting then or whether my interest was due to the fact that about that time I suddenly discovered the world of letters, I cannot now tell.

It was F. P. Hocker, town superintendent of schools, who at last taught me to find satisfaction in mathematical studies and helped me to discover that pure delight in plane geometry which I recall as one of the pleasantest memories of my high school life. Mr. Hocker had an artificial limb, the straps of which squeaked when he moved and thus always betrayed his approach to delinquents. We boys generally called him "Cork-leg" in conversation beyond the reach of our parents' ears, or his. But we had real respect for him. He loved to lead the school in singing favorite songs, such as "On the Banks of the Wabash Far Away"—one that reminded him of his

Indiana boyhood. He would beat time with a long wooden blackboard pointer, a rapt expression on his leathery old face. It was his interest that made the Audubon schools among the first, at least in towns of its size, to employ a regular music teacher. Mr. Hocker also showed his initiative by installing the town's first telephone system and by erecting a corn-canning factory at the edge of town—all while he was attending to his chief occupation, the direction of the schools.

Miss Bilharz was the daughter of the town's leading storekeeper, who was chairman of the Methodist Board of Stewards ("Stuarts," I thought they were called), lived in the best house in town, and was later president of a bank. Emil Bilharz had one of those big, double general stores, one side of which was dominated by the exciting smell of new calico and gingham prints and had a long counter in front of high rows of shelves loaded with yard-goods, with revolving stools for shoppers along the counter; and the other was distinguished by the stronger mingled odors of such grocery products as coffee, apples, and cheese competing from their barrels and cases. In the back of the store was the clothing stock for men and boys, and hung from the ceiling were lanterns, tinware, rubber boots, and so on. There were also dishes, lamps, glassware, and other objects of that sort somewhere back there. And in a shed at the rear were drums of kerosene and gasoline. For a child the most fascinating corner of the store was the one in which the glass-covered candy-case stood, with its chocolate drops (cone-shaped, nougat covered, with a thin coat of chocolate), its licorice in long black strings, its tiny red-hots, its brightly striped curled candy—such a delectable treasure hoard—and our pennies were hot in our fists! Townsfolk usually stayed away from Bilharz's on Satur-

days, for then the great "emporium" was thronged with
the farm trade, visiting, talking crops, and carefully shop-
ping. Bilharz's Store was an institution, famed the county
over.

In the small towns I knew in the nineties and around
the turn of the century, there were usually one or two
general stores, and in addition at least one all dry-goods
store, a clothing store or two, and a couple of smaller
groceries competing with the big general store. Each of
the groceries had its own delivery wagon, driven by a
clerk in regular hours and by a hustling boy after school
and on Saturdays. There were often two drugstores,
stocked not only with the standard items of the pharma-
copoeia but also with stationery, schoolbooks, and notions;
the old-fashioned ones displayed in their show windows
glass containers filled with colored liquids (I long wondered what magic philters these were, and it was a disappointment to learn that they were only colored water),
while the more progressive druggists would fill their front
windows with brushes and combs, fancy soaps, and even
books. Most of us had a nagging suspicion of all druggists because it was common knowledge that some of
them dispensed more Old Crow and similar beverages
than calomel, quinine, or ipecac. Soda fountains in drugstores were an innovation in the late nineties, though
there were ice-cream parlors in connection with restau-
rants.

Just off the corner of the Square was the butcher-
shop, with beef and pork carcasses hanging on hooks
along the wall, sawdust on the floor, and the butcher with
blood-stained apron at work by his chopping block behind the counter. In a county-seat town there were likely
to be a couple of such shops. Two or three times a week
Father would come home from the office at noon bringing

ten cents worth of beefsteak done up in butcher's paper,
a heavy, coarse, brown wrapping to soak up the oozing
blood; there was enough of the meat in such a purchase
for our family of six. Sometimes I would be sent down
to the butcher-shop for a five-cent soup-bone for our big
Saturday meal. When Father bought the Sunday roast
for twenty-five or thirty cents, the butcher would throw
in a nice piece of liver free.

Then there was a hardware store; it might also handle
agricultural implements, or another concern might take
care of the latter trade. If so, the implement store would
be just off the main street, so it would have room to display in a shed or out in an open lot next to the sidewalk
its gaily painted green and yellow and red wagons and
plows, harrows and hayrakes. Nearby was the lumber-
yard, with its long shed sweet with freshly-sawed pine.

But let us return to the Square. By the end of the
nineties, there was in every small town a "racket store,"
forerunner of the later five-and-ten; and often a little
jewelry and watch shop, which carried a small stock of
rings, gold pens, and so on. The furniture dealer, who
would also order pianos from Des Moines, doubled as
undertaker. Stuck in somewhere was a harness shop,
redolent of new leather, with the harness maker busy in
the rear with his awl and thread. The only harness maker
I ever knew well loved conversation, and he had a few
cronies who would sit with him for hours every day discussing in their slow way many things, old and new, far
and near. Talk would go on all day long, six days a week,
while D. E. Soar, the harness maker, would cut and shape
and sew, interrupted infrequently by the entrance of a
customer.

I must not forget the milliner. Her store might be
open only seasonally, for most women concocted their

own hats from materials bought at the other stores; but in the spring there was a rush of business, and the proprietress had to employ a bevy of assistants to make up new hats to order or to "make over" old hats for her customers. Gossips whispered that these "trimmers" were flibbertigibbets and not to be trusted too far.

There were no chain stores, except in the lumber business. Brand goods, which were soon to revolutionize merchandising everywhere with their special packaging, backed by intensive promotion, were not prominent in the stocks of small-town merchants in the nineties. There were a few clothing trade-marks that were well known, such as the W. L. Douglas $3 Shoe and Plymouth Rock $3 Pants, and also R & G Corsets (and others) for the women, and Ferris Waists for the girls. Quaker Oats was supplanting bulk oatmeal by the later nineties, supported by a national advertising campaign. Gradually the great flour manufacturers were pushing their products in and driving the local mills out of business. Royal Baking Powder, in its red cans marked "Absolutely Pure," Baker's Breakfast Cocoa, and Arm and Hammer Soda in packages were standard. Soaps (Pears', Ivory), cleaners (Sapolio, Pearline), and tobaccos (Horseshoe plug) were prominent brand goods in the nineties. Of course patent medicines had been necessarily trademarked and packaged for a hundred years and more.

But in the stores that I knew as a boy, we bought most things in bulk—sugar, salt, coffee, lard, dried fruits, or cookies. Canned peaches were a luxury, but most of our households "put up" enough fruit in season to last through the winter and spring. The women made their own dresses, coats, and lingerie; and the dry goods in greatest demand were yard-goods, ribbons, thread, buttons, etc.

On Saturdays, and on rainy summer days when work

in the fields was impossible, the stores and streets of the town would be crowded with slow-moving, visiting crowds, in which townsfolk mingled. Father would occasionally bring some friends from the country home to dinner on Saturday, but usually those who came from some little distance for a day in town expected to lunch off a dime's worth of cheese and free crackers. Very few farm families would go to the restaurant or hotel for the extravagance of the twenty-five-cent dinner, though stockmen commonly did.

There were hitching facilities along Main Street and around the Square. Teams were almost never put up at the livery stable but were fed from corn or oats brought along in the back of the rig or wagon, and they were watered at the town trough. Dust was inches deep in the streets in midsummer, and the town sprinkling-wagon brought welcome relief both downtown and in the residential districts; this service was supported by the subscriptions of the merchants and the citizens served. In wet weather, there was no such defense against the mud, which was everywhere, so that in a bad season it took good driving to avoid getting stuck in the middle of Main Street.

Some farmers—especially the young bloods—liked to frequent the barbershops and perhaps play pool on the tables kept in a back room. Some with a taste for rough conversation and whisky would hang about the livery barn. There were saloons in What Cheer when I was a young child there; it had begun as a coal-mining town, and the "wet" element was strong enough to defeat the "drys" in a state allowing "local option" but dominated by a prohibition policy. But in the more typical Iowa towns in which I lived later, liquor was procurable only from drugstores or bootleggers or from supplies laid up on occasional visits of friends to Chicago or Kansas City. Yet there was always the town drunkard. Old Briggs, once a law partner of the famous Benjamin F. Butler, now and then would stop a half-frightened boy to recite to him long passages from the *Aeneid* in hiccupped Latin. "Where on earth does Old Briggs get his whisky?" people asked. But cheap liquor was often to be had around livery stables and poolhalls. There was also a good deal of drinking by some people on festival occasions, as though red figures on the calendar were invitations to intoxication. Thus there was some drunkenness on the Fourth of July, Christmas, New Year's, at weddings, and during county fair week; but this was not general.

The town's hotel was something apart from a boy's life. Patronized chiefly by "drummers," it existed on the periphery of the community. It sent hacks to meet arriving trains, mainly to pick up the salesmen and their sample-cases. The drays, with their heavy teams, also met the trains to transfer freight. In many towns there were two trains daily, one each way, and each arrival was always an exciting event—a highlight of the town's day. Children were sometimes allowed to "watch the train come in," though many parents disapproved the custom, especially for growing-up girls. The reason was that every "drummer" was believed to have bold eyes for a young girl and strange, seductive powers over feminine virtue. Besides the hotel, there was the restaurant, with two or three tables and a lunch counter, and a pervading odor of frying things. Houseflies, pests of all our homes in summertime, swarmed in the restaurant despite sticky flypaper everywhere. But here you could buy a big meal, with meat and vegetables and pie, for a quarter—if you had a quarter. I was fifteen before I ate a meal in a restaurant.

And I was twenty before I spent a night in a hotel or even ate a meal in such a grand place. But I did visit the fine Commercial Hotel at What Cheer—a two-story frame building—when I was seven or eight, to have my head examined. A traveling phrenologist had set up an office there for a few days, and Father took his whole family in to have their craniums "read" by the great man. I remember Father was told that his bump of caution was distinctive and that he should therefore change from journalism to banking; and though he often felt in later years that he should have taken the phrenologist's advice, he was by that time too attached to newspaper work to desert it. As far as I can recall Father never told me what aptitudes, if any, the "reading" of my cranium revealed; but I am inclined to think that the prognostications were not encouraging. Hotels, too, furnished temporary offices for the "traveling doctors" who long maintained schedules that brought them to the small towns once or twice a month.

Nor did the courthouse mean much to a boy except for its position as a rather awesome architectural display piece set in the Square. Occasionally I visited the county auditor's office to collect the bounty paid for the tails of gophers another lad and I had brought up out of their holes by pouring in water at one end and catching them in a noose as they emerged at the other. And once, because the young defense lawyer was a neighbor, I was permitted to edge my way into a crowded courtroom to listen to the final argument in a murder trial.

The young lawyer was George Cosson, who later married my teacher Jennie Riggs and in the course of time became Iowa's attorney general. When I was in high school, George took time for long conversations with me, and I found his independent mind a great stimulus. "You will never benefit from school work," he told me one day as we walked along the wooden sidewalk on one of Audubon's shaded streets, "unless you become emotionally concerned. You have to be excited about geometry or you'll not do well in it." Of course, the doctrine was as old as Plato, but it was new to me then and seemed very wise. After many years of trying to use the principle in teaching, I still think it wise; but I have learned painfully that whatever a teacher may do to create such excitement, there is little hope for a student who is unwilling to dig deeply enough below the surface of a subject to find for himself the gold of a passionate interest in it.

In many a county-seat town, as I have suggested, the business district was built up around the Square, in the center of which the courthouse, the pride of the county, often displayed stone columns or even a dome. But in Audubon in my boyhood the Square was there all right; but every attempt to vote bonds to erect a fine courthouse was defeated by the southern part of the county, which stubbornly clung to the opinion that its town of Exira should be the county seat. It was a standoff; the northern two-thirds would not name Exira as county seat, and the south third stubbornly refused to give Audubon a courthouse. Meanwhile the Square remained a city park, with only a small bandstand in the middle of it; the county and court business was conducted in a rickety, big red-brick building east of the Square; and most business houses lined a main street running down hill to the westward.

That bandstand in the park was the scene of the Tuesday night concerts by the local band in the summer season. These concerts brought in evening crowds, stores remained open, people visited, children ran here and there squealing and shouting, young bloods from the country with their girls and fine rigs drove into town, ice-cream parlors did a rushing business. But town bands had a way of disintegrating after the season, losing their directors, failing to get merchants' donations for new instruments; and thus in most towns there were periods without so much as a fife and drum corps for the Fourth of July parade.

One group was always with us, inhabiting the benches in the city park or in the shade of the courthouse lawn. This was the "chin and chaw club" of old men, mostly retired farmers, who on every fine day forgathered to exchange reminiscences, talk politics, gossip about the misdoings of the younger generation, or just sit and chew tobacco, and occasionally spit.

The opera house, like the courthouse, was mainly outside my boyish purview. Our parents thought the strolling troupes and their offerings of melodrama and farce a bad influence, and on only four occasions in my boyhood did they yield to our pleadings to attend shows at the opera house. One of these was a hypnotist's exhibition, which had produced a sensation in the town and in which one of our printers was a predisposed and successful subject throughout the week's engagement. There was much laughter over the tricks which the hypnotized persons, who were well known to the audience, would be made to perform. But I found it all rather frightening, and especially so when one man under hypnosis was made rigid and laid down as a bridge spanning the distance between two chairs, his shoulders on the seat of one and his feet on that of another; then a big block of limestone was laid on his stomach and a man with a sledgehammer broke it in two with a mighty stroke—all without apparent harm to the subject.

More pleasant, and almost as thrilling, was the home-talent play, *The Union Spy*, the first dramatic production I ever saw. The role of the leading comic in this piece was played by a shoe clerk with the not inappropriate name of Hamm. As the story goes, this character, who was a very fat soldier, was captured by the Confederates and confined in Andersonville Prison, where he became a very thin soldier. (Hamm was naturally thin, but was well padded in the early scenes.) After his escape from Andersonville, he explains to the audience:

> They used to call me "Fatty Jones,"
> But now they call me "Skin and Bones."

For several nights those lines brought down the house, but the night we were there Mr. Hamm fluffed them. He got them started wrong: "They used to call me 'Skin and Bones,' " he began; and then, realizing there was nowhere to go from there—or scarcely anywhere—he finished in a burst of inspiration: "But now they call me—Nothing!" My father loved to recount this story, and always ended by declaring that it was one of the greatest examples of presence of mind he had ever observed.

Our parents relaxed the taboo against the offerings of traveling players when *Richard III* came to town. Was this not Shakespeare, and history to boot? So Father took us to the play on press tickets, and we saw the crookbacked Richard, heard him plotting evilly for the throne and arrogantly wooing Lady Anne. We wept over the young black-velveted princes in the Tower and their terrible fate, and we listened breathlessly to the ghosts: "Let me sit heavy on thy soul tomorrow!" We were thrilled by the midnight soliloquy of Richard in his tent, familiar to us from our father's reading of it at home. The marching and countermarching before the

battle, the orations of the leaders to their armies, and
finally the tremendous excitement of the duel between
Richard and Richmond kept us literally spellbound.
Father had to whisper to us that these were trick swords
with which they were fighting, that Richmond's weapon
did not really pierce the heart of the fallen king now lying
prone upon the stage. But it required the reappearance
of Richard in a curtain call to reassure us completely.

The other play by a touring company that we saw in
the opera house was *Uncle Tom's Cabin*. To youngsters
who had heard Mrs. Stowe's work read to them in infancy, this unseemly hodgepodge of farce and melodrama
was a disappointment. We laughted uproariously at
Marks; but we resented a little the introduction of Quakers
as comics, and the pathos was not successful.

The annual visit of the circus was a great event for
both town and country, for children and grownups. The
editor's children were never fearful of not getting into the
big show, because its press agent was always generous
with complimentary tickets. Mother never went, having
some Quakerish feeling of impropriety about it; but
Father was a circus fan and herded us through the
menagerie, bought peanuts for us, and sometimes even
indulged in tickets for the "concert" following the main
performance—which we were always so desperately
anxious to attend but invariably found so disappointing.

Less sensational but much more important were the
visits of lyceum talent to our town. The Lecture Course
furnished a series of cultural-social events which illuminated many long winters. These series of lectures, concerts, and dramatic readings were presented by groups of
guarantors, by church societies, by women's clubs, or by
any organization which the lyceum agency could induce
to accept the responsibility of selling tickets on a per-

centage basis. How important these lectures were to us is something it will be difficult to make the reader in this age of radio and television and automobile travel understand. We were much more isolated culturally than any small town can be today. A visit by Bishop McIntire, William Jennings Bryan, James Whitcomb Riley, J. Ellen Foster, or William Hawley Smith was something to be anticipated with delight and then recalled and talked over for weeks afterward.

I usually earned my admission to the lyceum events by distributing circulars throughout town about the coming attraction. It was not an easy job, but I was well paid when I listened enthralled to men like Henry Watterson and Robert J. Burdette. The first "lecture" I ever heard was mainly a series of readings from his own poems by Will Carleton. Of course he was not much of a poet, really; but how thoroughly we enjoyed "Gone With a Handsomer Man" and "Over the Hill to the Poorhouse"! He could make us laugh or weep, and his homely philosophy was very satisfying.

The circus, county fair, Fourth of July celebration, and Lecture Course brought together all elements of the townsfolk and the country people for miles around. Such gatherings illustrated the fact that ours was virtually a classless society. There were bankers and draymen, of course, and farmers and merchants, and Preacher McKee and Old Briggs. In many Iowa towns there were Catholic groups, which sometimes had elements of apartness. But there were no slums, and no areas on the wrong side of the tracks, as in more industrialized communities. On the whole, we were pretty homogeneous. If there was an upper, or dominant, class, it included perhaps a dozen men—the leading banker, the outstanding lawyer (perhaps a judge), a doctor who took an interest in public affairs, the owners of two or three of the biggest stores, the ministers of the largest congregations in town, the superintendent of schools, and the editor of the leading paper.

The banker requires special mention. Not only did he represent Money and Sound Credit in the community but he was often as much a personal adviser in family matters as was one's pastor or doctor. He was consulted by the father who was debating whether or not to send his boy to college, by the old man who was thinking of taking his wife on a trip to California, and by the widower who wanted advice about marrying again. Of course customers needing loans confided to him the stories of their misfortunes or their hopes for expansion of their various operations and all such matters, often in intimate detail.

Following the rural pattern of our community, our small industries were definitely countrified. Our butchers bought stock off the farm, for example, processed it at the slaughterhouse on the edge of town, and sold the meat from the carcasses at their shops.

The mill also bought neighboring farmers' products—corn, wheat, buckwheat—and ground them into flour, meal, and "shorts" for townspeople, for the producers on a grist basis, and sometimes for a modest city trade. How we used to look forward to the first fresh corn-meal of the autumn! Mush was our staple supper diet throughout the fall and winter. It was easy to prepare and said to be highly nourishing, but we became rather tired of it, even when it was covered with sorghum molasses. Too, the meal became stale and musty after a year; so as soon as we learned that farmers had brought the first corn of the new harvest to the mill and small quantities of fresh meal were available, Mother would hurry my brother and me off, with a flour-sack and a half-dollar, to visit the miller in his dusty, shaky, noisy old mill and get a supply of the tasty new crop.

The blacksmith worked chiefly for the farmers, shoeing their horses and repairing their implements. But the townsfolk had horses, too, and things to repair. One of my very early memories relates to a visit that I made at the age of six or seven to the blacksmith shop in What Cheer to have a hoop made. In our neighborhood all of the children were getting rolling-hoops—and with each the propelling "stick," a short iron bar attached to the hoop itself by a closed loop at its end. My father gave me the large sum of twenty cents to buy one, and I found the adventure of ordering it myself, and seeing it made, as much fun as rolling the new hoop home. The cindery, horsey smell of the shop, its dim interior in which the taciturn, leather-aproned smith found a long iron rod from which he cut a length for the job in hand, the bright red glow of the iron as he welded the ends together, with sparks flying: these things are still clear in my memory. The town had a tinner, too, who had his shop in the rear of the hardware store and turned out special pans and utensils for the housewife, stovepipes, pails, and such like.

The creamery was another local industry which served farmer producers. Owned co-operatively by the farmers, most of its product was shipped to out-of-town markets. Shortly after the turn of the century, factories for canning sweet corn were set up in many small towns in Iowa, but most of them did not last long. I worked in a canning factory one summer.

Creameries and dairymen could not do much business selling their products to local consumers because nearly every family kept a cow. My father bought some feed at the mill and had a farmer fill our haymow every summer, but we furnished some fodder for bossy from our garden.

Father also bought pasture rights in a communal field two or three blocks from our home where other families had their cows. Then throughout most of the year, morning and evening, my brother or I with a milk pail would trudge out to the pasture, halter bossy, and tie her up and milk her. On a warm summer evening, there is nothing so penetratingly hot to a boy who is doing the milking chore as the flank of a large yellow cow and nothing so vexing as the lashing of a cow's tail in flytime. We raised chickens, too, of course. Much of their feed came from garbage—an unknown word to us; we said "chicken-feed" or "slop." Many of our neighbors kept a pig in a pen in the backyard. We had one when we lived in What Cheer—a cute piggy in infancy, but he grew big and fat as his kind do, and he squealed so when the men took him away to the slaughterhouse that he broke our hearts. We never had a pig after that. Anyway, there was some talk about pigpens in town not being entirely sanitary; certainly most of them were malodorous.

Many of us were, in a way, small farmers. We surely raised big gardens. In my family, each of us had an individual section of the family garden for his own; and though the general plan came from our parents, each child had his own responsibility and his own pride in what he grew in his plot. I acquired at that time a passion for gardening that has been with me all my life. I came to regard raising vegetables as a creative art—something dreamed up and followed through from seed catalog to dinner table. To see the seeds I have planted breaking through the ground has for many years brought a new excitement with every recurrent spring and summer. Hoeing in my garden has seemed to me a calm and philosophic exercise, useful and healthful and mildly relaxing and satisfying. And picking the first succulent

green peas, bringing to the house the first fat red toma-
toes, snapping off the first roasting ears: these are the
climax of the year for the kitchen gardener.

And as far as household conveniences were concerned,
we were little better off than the farmers. We got hard
water from our own wells and soft water from our cisterns
or from rain-barrels set under the roof-spouting. We
had no plumbing: we used the primitive backhouse for a
toilet and a tin tub set on the kitchen floor for our Saturday night baths. We had no electricity in our house until
after the turn of the century, and then the lighting came
from globes attached to drop-cords. Electrical appliances
came into our home very slowly indeed. No telephones,
no central heating, no electric refrigeration in the nineties
—such novelties had to await the coming of the fabulous
twentieth century. Our icebox was just that: a nickel's
worth of ice shared space with perishable foods. Ice was
supplied from wagons which distributed it from house to
house in the hot weather. Children would pursue those
wagons through the streets begging for the crystal-cold
pieces which the friendly iceman would chip off when
he hewed out the five-, ten-, and fifteen-cent blocks for
the housewives. The cutting, storing, and distributing of
ice was an important local industry. My memories of
skating in zero weather on the creek at the bottom of our
town are tangled with pictures of men and teams cutting
ice and hoisting the great blocks into the big ice-house on
the creekside.

And so we were rural in many ways. Our little town
was part of the country landscape, nestled in the green
pastures and woodland, the crop-bearing fields. From
almost anywhere in town a walk of fifteen or twenty
minutes would take us out into a country road.

Well, all this was more than half a century ago. We

still have small towns in the Middle West, but they are different. They have been transformed by three factors: the agrarian revolution, which has reduced the importance of the small farmer with his independent operation (and now bids fair to eliminate him); the coming of the automobile, good roads, and electronic communication, which have shattered the walls of isolation that used to surround the rural communities; and the growth of brand marketing and pressure selling, which have not only ruined the primitive general-store system but have brought modern living in the small towns into step with that of urban communities.

Nobody wants to go back to the old times, but some precious things have been lost along the road to the new day. The chief loss, I think, has been that of the independent, self-reliant spirit that was once the central characteristic of the agricultural community. It was sometimes a prickly thing and hard to deal with, but there was a fine American integrity about it. It is not entirely gone, of course; but inside toilets, bathtubs, electrical appliances, and canned goods have not only "civilized" the small town but have conditioned it for the acceptance of our modern enveloping "mass culture" in exchange for the tough old self-reliance.

But this is old man's talk. It is not easy to recall to a just and equitable bar of memory the life and institutions of one's boyhood, and recollection sometimes spreads too rosy a hue over the past. One's eyes were keener and more roving in those days, the taste of an apple was more pungent on one's tongue, and every day brought new and exciting experiences. This is, after, all, a personal chronicle; and perhaps what I have been saying in my little essay about the small towns of the nineties is that once upon a time I was a boy in three of them.

3

The Old Printing Office

WE CALLED IT A "COUNTRY" printing office, because its
chief output was a "country" newspaper. Nowadays we
talk of the "community" newspaper. The word "country"
is now applied mainly to hillbilly music and a curious
kind of fellow known as a "bumpkin" or a "hayseed."
Like the words "villain," "boor," and "churl," all of which
originally meant countryman or farmer, the word "country" itself seems to have descended in the scale of re-
spectability. The philological standing of his word-
symbol appears to have followed the downward curve of
the countryman's economic status.

My father was not ashamed to call himself a "country"
editor: he was proud of the designation and the vocation.
He hoped I might follow in his footsteps; and in recom-
mending such a career to me when I was a boy, he said
that it had been his observation that, except for an occasional rascal or drunkard, the editor was always looked
up to in his small community. It might not be a big
puddle, Father said, but the editor was always one of the
big frogs in it. I think that was true. Whatever hierarchy
of leadership the country town possessed held assured
places for the editors—or at least one of the editors of the
two or three local papers. The editor was usually a political oracle; and he was sometimes sent to the legislature

or appointed to a state office. He was actually a liaison bringing the outside world of events and situations together with the life of the home community. He was supposed to be the best informed man in town on questions of the day. "They expect the editor to know everything," said my father; and he added, "You must get a good college education."

Father always regretted that he had never gone to college, but he made up for the lack of such training by the cultivation of studious habits throughout life. He was a tall man, standing six feet two, and of spare figure. He wore a full beard, dark red, which in its prime lay luxuriantly on his breast; as he grew older, he trimmed it more closely, until in his old age it was a white Vandyke.

A quiet man, Father always controlled his strong feelings about anything. Mother claimed that she had once heard him swear: it was when he was cleaning out a well and was surprised to discover a lost log-chain at the bottom of it.

"What did he say?" I once asked Mother.

"Better forgotten," she replied. "I don't want thee learning bad habits."

But I had never heard Father utter a profane word, and I persisted. Finally Mother confessed, in a shocked undertone, that on that famous occasion he had exclaimed, "Great Scott! It's the old log-chain!"

Father was thoroughly honest and just. I think he never told a lie; he could not even engage in a game of innocent deception without completely giving himself away. Yet he was in the thick of politics most of his life. He represented his county in the state legislature for a term or two and later served for a number of years on Iowa's Board of Parole.

The plant from which he issued his weekly newspaper

and in which he conducted a job-printing business consisted of a "front office" and a "back office." The former was much the smaller and was devoted to editorial and management activities, and the latter contained the mechanical department. In most midwestern towns in the 1890's the printing office was all in one room; and that was chiefly because the editor and manager was himself a printer and carried his editorial sanctum with him while he worked at the case or the press. Entering the front door of such an office, one walked directly into a fascinating confusion of characteristic smells, sounds, litter, and orderliness within disorder. But in our shops there was always a "front office," because Father had never learned the printer's trade; and besides, he liked a measure of privacy for conferences with visitors, for business transactions, and for the preparation of his copy.

Father often said he was sorry he had not gone into the "back office" for a while before he bought his first paper, the *What Cheer Patriot,* so he could have learned the mechanical side of the country newspaper business. Probably it was as well that he had not done so, for many a country paper in those years suffered from the editorial inattention of a proprietor who was kept busy getting out rush jobs of letterheads and sale-bills. But I am glad that he insisted on my learning the printer's trade in my boyhood, for it is good for anyone to have a mechanical trade, whether he uses it for a long or a short time.

I set my first type in the office of my father's *Tipton Advertiser* in 1896, when I was ten years old. My first copy was a piece of reprint credited to "Ex." to indicate that it had been taken from some paper obtained by "exchange"; and it probably had bounced around among many papers before Father had clipped it from one of his own "exchanges." It was a bit of verse with "run-in" instead of broken lines, dealing with a man's troubles in the spring, from housecleaning, wet feet and colds, too much gardening, and so on, in which every stanza (paragraph) ended with the plaintive plea: "Listen to my tale of wo!" It took me three or four evenings, working after school, to get this masterpiece of wit into pica type. I had almost finished the second stickful when, in my awkwardness, I dropped the whole thing on the floor. The printers laughed, thinking that now the boy was getting his first experience with pi; but when I scrambled down off the high stool to pick up the remains, I found the type intact in the stick! I had not learned to justify my lines properly, but had forced thin spaces in so that every line was very tight; indeed they were so tight that the type could scarcely be removed from the stick when it was ready for dumping on the galley.

I had plenty of experience with pi after that, however. Some years later, helping out in a rush hour when we were late getting to press, I removed my case, which was "poor" in type by that time, from the stand in order to shake it (a method of getting the remaining type out of the corners of the boxes and making it easier to pick up); but in my clumsy hurry, I dropped the entire case. There it was, pied all over the floor. I turned in dismay toward the foreman—and knocked a full galley of type ready for the forms off a galley rack. If I had not been the editor's son, I should have been booted out of the back door.

But usually setting type was, if not fun, at least mildly pleasurable. Monotonous it was, indeed, but there were always the twin challenges of speed and accuracy. On a Saturday, when cases were full and the office was clean and comparatively quiet after the hurly-burly of a Thursday press-day, followed by the "throwing-in" of Friday, when the type was returned to the cases—then it was that setting type was peculiarly satisfying. Beginning with a new case, the boxes rounded up full and the type cool and damp from fresh distribution, was a little like sitting down before a generously loaded table—just as working from an almost empty case, with dust at the bottom of the boxes, was like a starvation diet.

Sometimes the copy itself was interesting and instructive. I enjoyed setting up my father's editorial in bourgeois (pronounced berjoice); and I was always pleased when I found an excerpt from the current *McClure's* or *Harper's*, sent out by the magazine as promotion, on my hook. But how inexpressibly boresome was the monthly job of setting the patent medicine notices in nonpareil!

The principal machinery used by a country printing office in the nineties included eight or ten stands of type, a cylinder press, a couple of job-presses, and two or three imposing stones. The type stands and cases were of wood, and nearly always old and battered; it seems to me I never saw new printing equipment in my boyhood. We continued to use type long after it was badly worn, too, though our supply was sometimes replenished by those "foreign" advertising agencies which paid in printing materials instead of cash. Perhaps once in a decade a prosperous country weekly would come out in a "new dress" of brand-new body-type and fresh, sharp heads.

The newspaper press most commonly used was a flat-bed machine with a big tympan-bearing cylinder known as the Campbell. Because it was hand-powered and a stout man was required to turn the wheel on press-day, we nicknamed it the "Armstrong" press. We printed only the front and back pages, buying the sheets already printed on the second and third pages from the Western Newspaper Union in Des Moines. These "patent insides" were filled with miscellany suited to the small-town and rural audience, including farm and garden hints, a serial story, the Sunday school lesson, and a lot of advertising. The pages were generally large in the early nineties, but there was an increasing preference for a format with eight smaller pages, numbers two, three, six, and seven being "patent insides"; and still later there was such a strong movement to "all home print" that a few years ago the very last supplier of the "ready print" papers ceased and desisted.

The Gordon job-presses were not hand- but foot-operated. You gave the flywheel a turn, and then you kept the machine going by a foot-pedal as you stood in front of it feeding in blank sheets with one hand and removing the printed ones with the other. This we called "kicking off" a job. It was tiresome, especially with the larger jobber, and there was always some danger of getting a finger caught and crushed.

Steel is now used for the imposing surfaces on which the printer makes up his type forms, but in the days of which I write "the stone" was always made of stone, chipped around the edges perhaps, but very satisfactory for imposition. In later years, I found making up my own front pages in my own printing office one of the most interesting of a printer-editor's tasks.

My father called his group of employees "the force." It consisted of a foreman, two all-round printers, two lady compositors, and a "devil" who worked after school and on Saturdays.

At least, such was the personnel when my brother and I took turns "deviling" on the *Tipton Advertiser* in the mid-nineties. Our duties ranged from sweeping the floor and burning trash in the back yard to setting type and learning to feed the small jobber. Cleaning up after press-day was no easy task, for wastepaper, rags grimy with grease from the press, and dabs of sticky printer's ink seemed to be everywhere. Moreover, our job was complicated by the printers' habit of chewing tobacco. It was commonly said that printers were subject to lead poisoning because they were constantly handling type, which contains a considerable proportion of lead in its composition, and that the best antidote was chewing tobacco. This was probably a medical fable invented as an alibi by nicotine users; however, most printers chewed plug-tobacco, and the "devil" had to cope with their expectoration. We improvised spittoons from the heavy, small boxes in which we had received shipments of type and plates, filling them with sawdust and placing them conveniently near the type-stands, stones, and presses; but the chewers' aim was often imperfect.

Father was always particular about his foremen, and I remember them all as men of good character and some skill in "the art preservative of arts." Three papers that Father owned at various times he eventually sold to his foremen. He often had to take what he could get in the way of other printers, though, and they sometimes drank too much; indeed, I remember that we were often late with the first issues following the Fourth of July and Christmas because of trouble getting reorganized after the sprees that many printers regarded as their right on those holidays. I do not wish to wrong the average printer of those days: many of them were men of industrious habit and excellent character. My Uncle Artie worked in Father's printing office for several years; he was a fine, spruce young man who excited my unbounded admiration when he dressed up in approved bicycle costume—sweater, tight pants, and black stockings—in the evenings and rode a high-wheeler along the wooden sidewalks and dusty streets of What Cheer.

Our foremen were always strictly charged to see that the printers never annoyed or insulted the young women who set type for us, and who were themselves models of circumspect deportment. I well remember the two rather tall, buxom ladies who worked at adjoining cases in the back of our office at Tipton. Tightly corseted, wearing long skirts and shirtwaists with high collars under their aprons, with hair coiled high over artificial foundations known as "rats," they made an imposing and eminently respectable appearance.

Itinerant printers appeared once in a while, and sometimes, when job-work was plentiful, they were welcomed and put immediately to work. They came unannounced from nowhere, and they disappeared without warning into limbo. They had rainbows 'round their shoulders that lured them always to the next town or into the next state. "Tourist typos" my father called them. They usually brought some curious craft secrets with them—a new ingredient for our homemade blocking glue, a secret for a paste for "single wraps," or a formula for an ink to imitate embossing.

Usually these wanderers would stay with us no more than three or four weeks at the most, but I remember one man in his thirties who declared his intention to settle down and who stuck with us for over a year. He was a son of parents who were circus performers and he had been trained as a child aerialist; but a fall from a trapeze had injured his feet and turned him from the big tops to the printing office. He was tattooed all over the upper part of his body; and when he worked near the big window of the shop in the summertime with his shirt off for coolness, he drew such a crowd on the sidewalk and made such a scandal that a sleeveless undershirt had to be prescribed as minimum clothing. Whether this offended him, or whatever it was, one morning he simply did not show up. He left no debts behind him; indeed he had a couple of days' pay due him and he had paid his landlady ahead for board and room. Apparently the old wanderlust had carried him off between days. We never heard of him again.

Many of these "tramp prints," as we came to call them, were alcoholics. Either they drank because they were jobless or were jobless because they drank; probably it was the latter, since in those days of hand-set composition it was usually easy to get a "sit" in almost any town.

The climax of the week in the printing office was the Thursday press-day. The stress and strain, hustle and hurry of the weekly effort to "get out" on time brought the whole office to a high pitch of activity. Putting the last paragraphs of news in type picked from nearly empty cases, setting the last heads, correcting the galley proofs with swift care, marking and placing the corrected galleys for the make-up man—all of these things were parts of the planned urgency of press-day. What a welcome sound was the rat-tat-tat of mallet on planer which announced that the front-page form was ready to lock up in its chase! While the heavy form was being transferred to the bed of the press, we were laying clean papers on the stones and tables in readiness for the operation of hand-folding the edition. Also someone was preparing the patent mailer which (when it worked) addressed the folded papers; and another was laying out the wrappers for the single-list of papers to be dispatched to a distance. To help with the folding, the editor often recruited his whole family. My own mother, when her family was small, used to help fold papers on press-day. Some editors' wives worked so much in the office that they became practical printers, and occasionally one of these small plants was operated entirely by the editor's family. But on any paper, the tensions of press-day were bound to affect all the editor's family, and everyone helped as he or she could—with the news, the mechanical work, the folding, wrapping, and mailing, and the final carting of the papers to the post office.

I have been describing the old printing office as I remember it at the very end of the nineteenth century; and I realize I have been putting it all in a fixed status, as though it did not vary in place or in time. I write what I remember; but I know that there were many differences between various towns and the printing offices in them and that improvements took place from time to time. There were better towns, better offices, and better papers than ours, and many that were worse. Perhaps ours were fairly typical.

Changes came fast about the turn of the century. The greatest change was the adoption of gasoline engines to operate the presses. In 1898, my father, having bought the *Audubon Republican*, installed in its plant a new Country Babcock newspaper press, which would print two pages at a time, and put in a gasoline engine to power it. There was some skepticism in town on the question of whether such a sputtering contraption would actually run such a big press and run it evenly enough to print well; and there was also some resentment on the part of the muscular fellows who were thrown out of a Thursday afternoon job by the newfanglement. But it did work, under the careful nursing of Grif Wolf. Grif was the only man in town who really understood the mysteries of an internal-combustion engine; and on many a press-day afternoon he received an emergency call to hasten over to the printing office, where the press stood still while time was running out, and get that pesky engine started.

A few years later the line-casting machines began to revolutionize printing in the weekly shops. Before the casters came, however, Simplex Typesetters had been installed by some of the more daring publishers; but they broke type and made too much trouble. A primitive line-caster called the Typograph had some users. I operated one for some months. This machine had exposed wires down which the matrices slid to the assembly line when they were released by a heavy touch on the keys. When the line was complete, I turned a crank three revolutions to perform the casting operation, then tipped the whole fan-like top of the machine back so the "mats" would return down the wires to be ready for use in the next line. I never got so I could set much more on the Typograph than I could by hand. It was not until the Mergenthaler Linotype and the later Intertype came to dominate the field that mechanical composition became important in the country office.

The first casting machine I ever saw was a Mergenthaler on exhibit at the Trans-Mississippi Exposition at Omaha in 1898. My father took me with him on a two-day visit to this great fair; but the only things I saw there that I now remember clearly were the Linotype and an Igorrote village which had been transported bodily from the Philippines, complete with nearly naked natives. My observation of the Igorrotes was brief, though facinated; but I later spent a year operating a Linotype, and my life has had certain connections with that mechanical marvel ever since.

But that was when I was on my own. In the years when I was a boy in my father's office, our equipment was more rudimentary. We did not even have central heating at Tipton, and my brother and I had to bring in the wood to keep the fires in two stoves going all winter.

There was no typewriter in our office until Father traded advertising space for a primitive Blickensderfer in 1899, but he never learned to use it with facility.

The subscription price of the typical midwestern weekly during the nineties was a dollar a year. The rate was often quoted at a dollar if paid in advance and a dollar and a quarter when past due, but usually the editor was so glad to have the old account paid that he would throw off the extra quarter. The "delinquent" subscriber was the curse of the American weekly newspaper for more than two hundred years; but when an editor knew most of his thousand or so patrons personally, it was hard to strike off the list the names of any who fell a little behind. Besides, many farmers felt reluctant to pay for anything they had not received—which seems reasonable. I doubt if my father really lost a great deal in bad accounts. I remember his calling me into his office one day and showing me a pile of ten silver dollars on his desk. "Ole Olsen, from the southwest corner of the county, was just in and paid his subscription," Father said; and added, "I thought you might like to see it sometimes pays to trust a man. I knew Ole would be in sometime. He is all right—just a little slow." Ten years slow.

The advertising rate on our paper was eight cents a single-column inch in the nineties, but Father raised it to ten cents just about the turn of the century. That made it cost three dollars to insert a quarter-page "ad." Most of the advertising was paid for at the end of the month, or, in the case of transient business, in advance; but there were a few large accounts that were settled annually. With those few stores we ran a year's bill on which our parents charged purchases, while the merchants would let their own advertising and job-work bills pile up. Settling such accounts on the day following New Year's was very exciting for the family. Since we were always careful to keep the balance on our side, Mother could at these times get the yard-goods she wanted for new dresses, my brother and I got new shoes, and there were always settling-up treats of candy.

Most country editors provided a column or two of "editorials." These articles and paragraphs were usually written with care and read with respect. Later consolidations, which have commonly left only one paper in a town, have had a tendency to prevent participation in controversies; but sixty years ago, when every town worth its salt had at least two newspapers, sides were always vigorously taken. The rival editors often engaged in bitter quarrels. Those battles in type were frequently carried too far and were filled with personal attacks, invective, and intemperance, but they stimulated reader-interest in editorial columns and perhaps sharper thinking about issues. Unrestrained scurrility and personal attack were perhaps more common in the pioneer press; but in the nineties there were still editors who loved to print innuendo and even outright accusation regarding the characters and private lives of their "contemporaries" of the opposing party, all in fancy writing adorned by such epithets as "poltroon," "blackguard," "the miserable slang-whanger who edits the filthy sheet which disgraces our fair city." It is easy, however, to overemphasize the vulgarities of the fighting editors of those days; there were also many sober and respectable country Greeleys and Danas whose articles were read with quiet acceptance at home and quoted with approval abroad.

My father was a controversialist in his editorial column, especially on party matters; but he was never violent. On the whole, I think his editorials were too heavy, but they suited certain tastes of the times. Perhaps his very moderation and his sedulous abstention from invective sometimes provoked rival editors to excesses of attack; certainly there were times when he caught it hot and heavy. Father was a Republican by family tradition and by personal conviction. It seemed as though his Republicanism was a built-in element of his personality. "That galled and jaded wheel-horse of the Republican machine," the editor across the street once called him: I think Father rather liked that jibe.

Occasionally Father would with some effort strike a lighter note. The most famous piece he ever wrote was about a prayer he had heard a country preacher offer one Sunday. This was in the midst of the drought of 1898, in the time also of the Spanish-American War. Here is the prayer as Father set it down on his arrival at home and as he published it in his paper the following week:

. . . And O Lord, we ask for rain. Thou hast taught us to come to Thee to ask for what we need, and we need rain. Thy servants of old prayed for rain, and their prayers were heard. Elijah prayed for rain, and his prayer was answered. The ground is parched, the grass is dying, the heat oppresses us so we can hardly breathe. O Lord, give us refreshing rain!

We prayed for rain last week, and it has not come yet. Perhaps we did not need it as badly as we thought. Now the farmers say we will not have half a crop unless we have rain soon, but then some would say that anyway. But we know we need rain! O Lord, we need money to carry on this righteous war for humanity, and we need crops to get the money with; so, Lord, give us rain that we may have the crops.

Thou hast tempered the winds to our battleships. The typhoons and the hurricanes of the Tropics have not molested them. Thou hast given us the victory, and we praise Thy name. . . .

The story ended simply by telling how, as the editor drove home that afternoon, he noticed a cloud in the northwest "as small as a man's hand" and how that night the whole countryside received a generous downpour. This article was quoted in the *Des Moines Register*, picked up by other papers, and eventually reprinted all over the country.

Mother contributed a "Temperance Column" to our paper. She began it in the face of What Cheer's ten saloons, and later continued it in dry Tipton. Much of it—both prose and verse—was original, though some was carefully "selected." When I reached high school, I wrote weekly "School Notes" for the paper. We all gathered "items"; we were conscious of representing the paper wherever we went.

It has long been common for urban satirists to under-value the local news reporting of the small-town weekly. But that report and record has, in fact, certain great and fundamental values. Devotion to home is the first loyalty, the foundation of patriotism, a primary virtue. The country paper is dedicated to the homely matters—to births and deaths, the churches and the schools, crops and weather, the parties and bees of the home folks. William Smith has been painting his house; Mr. and Mrs. Richard Jones have been enjoying a visit from their son, Sam, who is doing so well in Cedar Rapids as an inspector in the new Quaker Oats factory; the Christian Endeavor will have an ice-cream social on the A. Y. Simmons lawn Thursday evening, with adjournment to the nearby church basement in case of rain. William Dean Howells once defined the realist as the writer who "cannot look upon human life and declare this or that thing unworthy of notice." The country editor was (and still is) a realist who is committed to the belief that such bits of life and social intercourse as are recorded in the "items" of his news columns make up an important sum of human living. And the record that he prints serves to unite and solidify community interests and community loyalty.

My father never thought his work trivial or of little consequence. We all looked upon our paper as the historian of many lives. We knew that we put town and country down in black and white—joys and sorrows, good and ill, peace and war, prosperity and failure. We watched the growth and development of the community, the decay of some institutions, the setting of new patterns. Our paper recorded all of these things, bringing our people and the little episodes of their lives and the town's events together within the compass of a few columns weekly. Thus any country paper welds together all the elements of its social group in a continuing history.

As I look backward at the country paper of the nineties and the first decade of the new century, it seems to me to have performed three services—in some instances badly, indeed, but in many very well. It was the contemporary historian of local events; it offered an editorial column that was often thoughtful and sometimes influential; it contributed to the economic welfare of its community by affording a good advertising medium and by acting as a leader in all progressive movements.

For many years now, everything in America has been irresistibly swept up into the prodigious heaps of the great cities and their sprawling suburbs. But some nine thousand newspapers remain to serve about that many small towns throughout the nation. The weekly of to-day, however, is not the same country paper I knew as a boy; it has a Linotype, it is illustrated by local pictures, it is smarter, it serves its advertisers better, and it sells for from two to four dollars a year. Nor is the town it serves the same, as I have already tried to show in my essay on the country town of my boyhood; it is no longer a semi-isolated hamlet, undisturbed by the blare of automobile horns, unstirred by the incursion into its midst of the strange phantasmagoria of "show business" on electronic screens in every home.

But in spite of changing patterns, the home paper of today has the same spirit of neighborliness and service that it has always had, and it continues to integrate the life of its community. It was the object of my fascinated devotion throughout my early life, and I have never lost my deep interest in it. The local editor, the country printing office, and the home-town paper have played a vital part in many lives through many years.

4

An Amateur Reader

I AM BOOKISH AND HAVE BEEN so since childhood. Fault
or virtue, there it is. *Ich kann nicht anders.* I like to
think it is a virtue; at any rate it is a necessity, and I might
as well try to make a virtue of it.

I read for new ideas, for information and instruction,
for the delights of fancy, for pleasures of style, for mere
amusement; often to keep up with current movements,
sometimes to stimulate a slothful mind, or, on the other
hand, to find relaxation. And this diversity of aims in
reading is naturally matched by the variety of books
read. From laborious works of philosophy to the latest
mystery story, from Plutarch to Harry Golden, they are
all grist for my mill.

Sometimes I read an old book just because I am
ashamed never to have read it before. Justice Holmes
once wrote to Sir Frederick Pollock: "I hate to give up
the chance to read this and that, that a gentleman should
have read before he dies. I don't remember that I have
ever read Machiavelli's *Prince*—and I think of the Day of
Judgment." Later in his letters to faithful Pollock, he
occasionally told of reading something or other "for the
Day of Judgment." I have recalled this bon mot of the
old Justice many times since I read it some twenty years
ago. Indeed, I have taken it so to heart that I have

imagined myself applying for admission at the Golden Gate only to hear St. Peter ask in awful tones if I had read some antique classic or other.

St. Peter: Have you read *Lavengro?*
Trembling Shade of Me: Well, no; not officially, so to speak. I've read *about* it——
St. Peter: Out! Begone! Depart into outer——

What about this *Lavengro*, anyway? My bookstore did not have a copy; the clerk said there was no demand for it. At the library, however, I found Borrow's eccentric masterpiece, dusted it off; my wife and I read it aloud and found it good.

But this sounds like duty reading, and that I am quite against. To be sure, there must be some kind of forced labor in preparation for barbarous examinations, in perusing an unwelcome book one has promised to review, and even in reading some dreary, repulsive thing in order to find out, if possible, why some critics have praised it. But by and large and in the main, reading should be done for one's personal pleasure. Intellectual stimulation is one of the highest gratifications. Reflective or sportive fancy in poetry or essay is enchanting. The thrills of romance recreate and rejuvenate a reader's faculties, unless they are too curdled by the rennet of austere criticism and intellectualism.

The first book I ever wrote for a regular publisher was one, now quite forgotten, called *Rewards of Reading*. As I look over it today, I find it rather sophomoric; but it has zest and gusto, and from beginning to end it stresses the idea of personal pleasure in reading. "Your reading must be exceedingly personal to *you*," I wrote, with italics. "Its success will depend upon what *you* find of pleasure in it." And I had a good sharp quotation from

Montaigne: "If one shall tell me that it is to degrade the Muses to make use of them only for sport and to pass away the time, I shall tell him that he does not know the value of that sport and pastime so well as I do."

Much of that "sport and pastime" derives from the adventure of reading a book that is new to one. One may have read reviews of it, but what bamboozlers and deluders reviewers often are! Or, to put it more kindly, what is true for them may be quite false for me. I must find out for myself. And so I go adventuring within the pages of a new book with a sense of exploration in a strange country. I may be disappointed, or I may make wonderful discoveries—but always when I open the pages of a new book I enter upon a fresh adventure.

Few pleasures compare with the delight of acutely personal literary discovery. "What's this?" I exclaim when I come upon an exciting passage or page, essay or poem, in some unlikely place. "Why, this is literature!" Then I go on with a "second take," and I roll the morsel over my tongue. "Literature? Well, it tastes like it, feels like it. . . ." But what is literature? Something that makes the heart beat faster? Something that moves one deeply and keeps one thinking and seems to answer, however subtly, the fundamental question of what life really means? Something that sticks in one's mind and seems, on enthusiastic re-reading, to have perhaps a certain predictability for what we call "permanence"? Or at least to be worth recalling and talking to my friends about? I give it up. I cannot define literature in unacademic, personal terms; but I have known repeatedly the delight of coming unexpectedly on some bit of writing that has given me a heart-stopping sense of something marvelous—if not from a peak in Darien, then from my armchair with a book in my hand.

I do not remember what were the first books I ever read. I think we had a *Mother Goose* in our home, and of course there were the school readers—not McGuffey's, alack, but something more diluted. I somehow missed the various series of juveniles, except for *The Five Little Peppers and How They Grew*, with its sequels, which a grade-school teacher read aloud to "the Room" day after day in the morning reading period. She liked them, and we were not quite disinterested. But throughout my boyhood I had a snobbish contempt for books written down to children. When I was in the ninth grade, I broke a leg in a coasting accident, and one of my teachers came to our house to see me and left me the gift of a book by G. A. Henty. Now the Henty books were fine, I am sure; but I could have wept because she had not brought me something better than a "kid's book." *Hans Brinker* was a delight, however, and the Alcott stories were absorbing: these seemed less childish. I was given a copy of *Pilgrim's Progress* one Christmas by a mistaken friend who thought it a children's book; its pictures were interesting, but I found the text hard going.

But blessed was the *Youth's Companion,* with its tales in series by the immortal C. A. Stephens, all founded upon true incidents of his own youth in Maine. What fun! What salty characters! Of course, there was much more than Stephens in the "Yousipanen," as the little ones, eager for "The Children's Page," called it. There were continued stories by Sophie Swett dealing with family life, and better than the Alcott stories, we thought; stories of boys in sports by Arthur Stanwood Pier; and wise, anecdotal pieces by famous men like Grover Cleveland, Edward Everett Hale, Theodore Roosevelt, and a host of others. And there was a matchless page of curious little amusing stories in fine print, each prefaced by a brief moral "application" which we soon learned to skip in spite of the editor's lure of larger type for those homiletic prefaces. How we hurried home from school Monday noons, each of us hoping to be the first to seize the beloved paper and get a quick, excited look at what we were to enjoy during the week! In October came the great "Premium List Number," with its illustrated catalog of all kinds of wonderful things that could be obtained free for one, two, three, ten new subscriptions—scroll saws, magic lanterns, small printing presses, tools, Bibles, atlases, books singly and in sets, dolls for the girls, and so on. I was never a good salesman; but I once obtained one new subscription and chose for my prize a two-volume life of Lincoln, by Henry J. Raymond. It proved to be one of the dullest books I ever read.

St. Nicholas was a welcome monthly visitor, every page of which we studied eagerly. Kipling's "Mowgli" stories, tales by Stevenson, Mark Twain's *Tom Sawyer Abroad,* some of them read aloud in the family circle, were pure enjoyment; and Palmer Cox's "Brownies," forerunner of the more blatant newspaper comics, were fascinating. But again I am getting ahead of my story, for I wish to reserve my early preoccupation with magazines for a later chapter.

Ours was a great family for reading aloud. The love of reading bound us all together as firmly as the ties of blood. This, of course, was because our parents had a quiet passion for literature which they imparted to their children. I have already told how Father and Mother were brought together in a Friends' boarding school by sharing the reading of a "bootlegged" single-volume Shakespeare. It was from that same blue-and-gold volume that Father used to read to us all on Sunday evenings. His favorites were *The Merchant of Venice* and *The*

Tragedy of Richard the Third. Early in his life at What Cheer, he had once participated in a "home talent" production of *The Merchant*, taking the very minor role of Tubal; and this experience had given him a special interest in that play. He had a good, deep voice, and he loved to emphasize what he called the "circumflexes" in the ironical speeches of Shylock:

> Fair sir, you spi-it on me on Wednesday last;
> You spu-urned me such a day; another time
> You called me daw-awg; and for these *cour-te-sies*
> I'll lend you thus much mo-onies?

I cannot reproduce it in print, but how firmly it is all fixed in my memory! Nor can I forget the eerie hollowness of Father's voice when he read the midnight soliloquy of Richard:

> The lights burn blue. It is now dead midnight.
> Cold, fearful drops stand on my trembling flesh.

Ossian was another favorite of Father's; he had bought the volume as a present for his bride when they were on their wedding journey. The orotund periods and florid imagery of that once popular work thrilled us when Father read the poems aloud in the family circle:

Whence is the stream of years? Whither do they roll along? Where have they hid, in mist, their many-colored sides? I look into the times of old, but they seem dim to Ossian's eyes, like reflected moonbeams on a distant lake. Here rise the red beams of war! There, silent, dwells a feeble race! They mark no years with their deeds, as slow they pass along. Dweller between the shields! thou that awakest the failing soul! descend from thy wall, harp of Cona, with thy voices three! Come with that which kindles the past: rear the forms of old, on their own dark-brown years!

Father's own reading was mostly in history and biography. In spite of his constant preoccupation with his business and with politics, he read steadily through Gibbon's *Decline and Fall,* McMaster's *History of the People of the United States,* and other such works. He had little taste for fiction. Once a lecturer on our winter lyceum course declared that *Les Misérables* was the greatest novel ever written; so Father bought a copy and plodded through it, but I think the only part he enjoyed much was the story of the Battle of Waterloo. He was not quite sure the book was adapted to my years; but he was right in allowing me to read it (indeed, he scarcely ever forbade me any book), for the tragic Valjean, the implacable Javert in the sewer tunnels of Paris, the bishop and his candlesticks, and of course Waterloo made a lifelong impression on me.

Mother's chief interests were in poetry and fiction. In her girlhood her own mother always gave her a volume of verse as a birthday gift; and, after she was married, Father continued that custom until her death. I have most of those books now, and they make an interesting collection. I think mother liked the woman poets best—Miss Ingelow, Mrs. Hemans, the Cary sisters, Mrs. Sigourney, and also (somewhat at a distance) Mrs. Browning and Christina Rossetti. Mother herself wrote much verse during her life. She was chiefly an "occasional" poet: no birthday passed for any one of us without stanzas in that beloved regular hand, and marriages of friends or births or deaths within the wide circle of her acquaintance brought forth graceful, intimate verses. Also she often wrote "pieces" for us to speak at school "rhetoricals" and church programs and then drilled us in their rendition. And I do mean to say that she drilled us; we had to practice over and over the proper tone, emphasis, expression

for each line, with appropriate gestures. I can never
express fully how much this careful training helped me
in public address later in life.

This is perhaps the place to say a word about that
wonderful, forgotten textbook-anthology *Kidd's Elocution*.
My parents both had studied it at boarding school, and
its fine old pieces remained a pleasure to them and became a delight to their children.

I cannot think now how she managed it, in that busy
household, but Mother did often read aloud to us,
especially when we were very young. Obviously, she
always found time enough to do what she felt it best
to do. The first book I remember hearing her read was
Uncle Tom's Cabin, but we cried so hard over poor
Eliza's troubles that she gave that up. Later she read to
us from *St. Nicholas* and from Longfellow and Whittier.
Evenings when Father worked late at the office, Saturday
afternoons when everything was "red up" for Sunday,
she would sit rocking in her chair as she read to us in her
strong, expressive voice while we sprawled about on the
floor listening to the magic lines of "Hiawatha" or
"Evangeline." It is the fashion today (in some circles)
to deride Longfellow, but his lines *were* magic then; and
the worn carpet and familiar furnishings, our family in-
timacy, and our mother's voice were magic, too.

But as we grew up a little, we no longer listened idly
while Mother read; we all engaged in some household
task except the reader appointed for the hour. There was
one summer when a big sweet-crab tree in our back
yard bore a tremendous crop, and Mother could not bear
to see its fruit go to waste; she must "put it up" in glass
jars; so we pared and cored crab apples and read Dickens
throughout long weeks of our school vacation. None of
us minded the monotonous work as long as we could

have *The Old Curiosity Shop* and *Nicholas Nickleby* to go with it. I remember that as the golden summer of Dickens and the crab apples.

David Copperfield I read by myself, mostly while lying out under some bushes at the edge of our garden. I was then in my early teens and was reading everything I could get my hands on. As Father prospered in business, he added considerably to our home library, buying many good secondhand books by mail bids through a New York auction concern. Also I was a constant patron of our Sunday school library; from its shelves I got most of E. P. Roe, and Scott and Miss Porter, and also *Fox's Book of Martyrs*—the latter a sadistic work I am not prepared to recommend to young or old. The only clandestine reading I can recall was *Trilby*, which I found as a serial in old *Harper's Monthly's*. Mother disapproved it, and I think I never told her that I read it out in our haymow—with fascinated interest and with no ill effects so far as I know. I read many things out in that haymow, including two or three volumes of Rollin's slow-moving *Ancient History* dealing largely with the Persian Wars. A little later, the Columbian Club, a women's study club of which my mother was an active member, set up a small library in an upstairs room off Audubon's main street, and from it I borrowed some elementary works on anthropology and biology.

When I was fourteen, my Grandfather Tipton died. He had been a farmer in Ohio and a poor man all his life. I had never seen him more than once or twice, but he was kind enough to leave me five dollars in his will. What to do with this windfall? I had no hesitation about it: I would lay it out in books—the beginning of a personal library. The local druggist, who was our only bookseller, allowed me to take home a catalog of A. C. Mc-

Clurg and Company, long the leading jobbers to the book-trade in the Middle West, so that I could choose my books carefully. I took pride in making up the list myself, without benefit of adult advice; but I have not the slightest idea today why I chose these particular books. Perhaps I had heard or seen them recommended. Here is the list:

> Carlyle's *French Revolution*
> Carlyle's *Heroes and Hero-Worship*
> *The Rubáiyát of Omar Khayyám*
> Froude's *Caesar*
> Bishop Quayle's *A Hero: Jean Valjean*

A substantial five dollars' worth. The *French Revolution* was bound in three-quarters leather, and the *Rubáiyát* (Fitzgerald's translation, of course) carried Gilbert James's illustrations backed by tint-blocks. Quayle's lecture was the only slight item among them, but it was attractively bound. Two of these books—the *French Revolution* and the *Rubáiyát*—cast over me a spell from which I have never emerged.

The eloquent narrative of Carlyle held me rapt: the storming of the Bastille, the slaughter of the Swiss Guards, the death of Robespierre on the guillotine. I still consider the sketches of individual characters—Marat, Mirabeau, Robespierre, King Louis, and others—to be the most brilliant gallery of portraits in literature. I remember following my mother about to the kitchen or to other rooms where her household tasks took her and begging her to listen while I read some glowing passage to her; I could hardly bear not to share these treasures. I know now that Carlyle has not always been in favor among the more academic historians, but his *French Revolution* was heady liquor to me as a boy; and I have retained through the years the conviction that, with all his rhetoric, the old philosopher-historian had and still has much to say that is worthy of our admiration and our study.

As for Omar, I committed all of those quatrains to memory in my high-school days, and I can still recall some of them word for word with pleasure. A little later, when I was a junior at Simpson College, I won the Badley Essay Prize with a screed pointing out parallels between the *Rubáiyát* and the Old Testament Book of Ecclesiastes; I think my success was mainly due to the fact that the essays had to be read aloud before an audience, and in declaiming mine I had a chance to spout the beloved lines to my heart's content.

I was sixteen when my father bought that great anthology called *The World's Best Literature,* in thirty-six substantial volumes. It was edited, nominally at least, by Charles Dudley Warner; and there was an introductory essay about each author represented, many of them by distinguished critics. In the next-to-the-last volume there was an analytical table of contents in which authors were arranged geographically; and I resolved to study the literature of the world on that basis, using this Warner library as a starting point, but extending my reading, whenever the extract was tempting, to complete masterpieces. That this was a lifetime program (perhaps more suited to two or three lifetimes) did not daunt my naïve ambition. And so I began with Africa, as the book said. I had enough of St. Augustine from the excerpts from *The City of God* in Warner; but when I came to Olive Schreiner, I read the whole of *The Story of an African Farm.* I read through Austria, Canada, and Denmark; but when I came to England I resorted to chronology, and I think I had not quite reached Chaucer when I left home for college. I never returned to the grand project.

In college my reading was deepened necessarily, and broadened, as I shall relate when I tell about some of my more inspiring teachers in another essay. And after all that, I found myself reading more in contemporary belles-lettres. I worked up a great enthusiasm for the midwestern school. I read John G. Neihardt's epic narratives of the West with mounting admiration, and one day I got on the train and went out to Bancroft, Nebraska, to see and talk with the poet; this began a lifelong friendship of much value to me. I discovered Vachel Lindsay in the pages of the old *Independent* and struck up a correspondence with him. For years I recited some of his audience-participation poems to groups of various kinds— "Daniel in the Lions' Den," "General William Booth Enters Into Heaven," "John L. Sullivan, the Strong Boy of Boston," and others. But the poet visited England in 1920, and transatlantic critics found "The Congo" too boisterous; they could not hear the voice of the social interpreter beneath the noise of the tom-toms and the mumbo-jumbo cries. So when I had Lindsay on an Iowa City platform a year or two later, he consented to read "The Congo" only on my insistence, and then he *whispered* it all, insisting that it was originally intended to be read that way.

I had similar enthusiasms for Hamlin Garland, whose work I had known since childhood and a collection of whose poems I was later to have the pleasure of editing for a limited edition; and for the group of *Midland* writers at Iowa City, with which I was eventually to become identified. I was excited by Edgar Lee Masters and his Spoon River characters, by the Grinnell sociologist Edward A. Steiner, and by many other writers who seemed to me to be making readers all over the country more conscious of the Middle West that I knew and loved.

In my high-school days I had been accustomed to write, for my private satisfaction, little pieces about books I had read and liked; and now I was able to publish short, appreciative essays about these Midwesterners I had "discovered" in my own weekly paper at Grand Junction, Iowa, and even to contribute a few articles about them to the magazines. Probably the percentage of interest among my *Globe* readers for these things was low and therefore they may have been bad journalism. When I sold my paper after a few years, editorial contemporaries in towns roundabout expressed the usual polite good wishes to a departing brother; but P. A. ("Pa") Smith, of the *Scranton Journal,* could not forbear adding to his farewell the mildly disapproving observation: "Mott is the literariest cuss that ever flashed across the Greene County horizon."

My dabbling in writing during the years at Grand Junction made me want to do more of it. I suppose I had always hoped to be a writer. At length I decided that the long and hurried days of a newspaperman's life gave little or no opportunity for such work; but if I could get into college teaching, I should then have plenty of leisure for both reading and writing. How wrong can a man be? At any rate, I sold my paper at a good deal more than I had paid for it; and with high hopes my wife and small daughter and I set off for Columbia University, where I was to perform graduate work that we hoped would lead to a teaching career.

There was much duty reading in those years during which I was concentrating upon the English language and literature, but also no little reading for pleasure, and often I could draw no line between the two. Even reading the fourteen large volumes of the *Cambridge History of English Literature,* though mostly a plodding business, was not without its satisfactions and rewards.

I ran low in funds during my last year at the university and found a job teaching in the Marquand School for Boys. This was a curious institution located in the Central Y.M.C.A. Building in Brooklyn. I have three pleasant memories of my work there—association with a few bright boys among the students, an acquaintance with Ludwig Lewisohn, who was also doing a stint of teaching at Marquand to replenish a slim pocketbook, and the reading I did on the long subway trips from home to work and back again.

Reading on the subway! It is an art and an adventure. I am not talking about reading the carefully folded newspapers in crowded cars, as nearly everyone does, but about reading books. We lived, at the time of which I write, in the New York Heights district in upper Manhattan, and the express made the run to Atlantic Avenue, Brooklyn, in about an hour. When I boarded the train at the Heights station, I had no trouble in finding a vacant seat, and I took out my book and began to read. A little later my car would be jam-packed with men and women holding to strap-handles, swaying, grasping briefcases, newspapers, and parcels, on their was to work downtown. But I read on unperturbed. It was much the same coming home in the late afternoon. On those subway rides, I read all of Emerson's works in the little blue and gold Riverside edition, handy for the pocket, as well as Will Durant's essays on the philosophers in the Haldeman-Julius "Little Blue Books," and many other things.

But it is easy for a subway reader to become so lost in his book that he suddenly finds himself transported into the Bronx or some other unknown district. One night after spending the evening on some project at the public library downtown, I started home on the subway. I remember I was reading the pre-Elizabethan tragedy *Gorboduc*. When I suddenly emerged from the turgid stream of the passions of Ferrex and Porrex some time later, I found to my dismay that I was somewhere in the Bronx; I had taken the wrong train at Times Square. I left the train and crossed over, got another express downtown, and resumed my reading. This time I was nearly as far as the Battery before I realized I had missed my proper change to an uptown train. I had finished *Gorboduc* before I reached home and an anxious family well after midnight.

In my years as a college and university teacher, much of my reading has naturally been in the descriptive and critical works dealing with my specialties, but I have nearly always enjoyed it. Biography and social history have always been favorite fields for my exploration, and for years I was a short story enthusiast.

And we still read poetry aloud at our house. In our earlier married life, my young wife shared my ardors about Neihardt, Lindsay, and the Midwesterners; but her discipline in the older fields had been more regular than mine, and it was she who introduced me to Wordsworth and Shelley, and others of the English romantics. My love for Wordsworth has been an enduring passion, and even now I cannot read again certain lines of the "Intimations" and "Tintern Abbey" without being moved almost to tears by their beauty.

We have shared lighter literature, too, including mystery fiction, in which we have common tastes. We became detective story addicts largely through reading Earl Derr Biggers and S. S. Van Dine. Of course, we had both read Conan Doyle and Mrs. Rinehart, but our doom was sealed by Mr. Moto and Philo Vance. We used to read a Van Dine story two-thirds through aloud, then each seal up a guess on the identity of the guilty one, and finish the book separately and quickly. Ah, welladay! And also alack! Too often we were both wrong!

On the faculty of the State University of Iowa in the late twenties, I knew several others, in various departments, who were fellow addicts of the anodyne puzzlers; and I conceived the idea of organizing twelve of us, with appropriate mystery, into a reading group to be called "The Campus Crime Club." The purpose was to get the best new mysteries promptly into the hands of the members. The titles I chose from the reports in the *Saturday Review of Literature,* and I made arrangements with one of the bookstores to handle the orders, make the collections (two dollars each six months), and attend to the distribution. Then I wrote eleven prospective members the following letter on cheap paper (such as may be purchased, as they say, at any stationery store), varying the name and form of address, of course, with each missive:

Mon cher Monsieur:

Your name is Hercule Poirot.

You are required to join a conspiracy.

On Thursday next, between the hours of 1 and 5 p.m., call at the Book Shop, wait until you can catch the eye of the proprietress, and then whisper in her ear the words: "I am Hercule Poirot." She will then deliver secretly to you a copy of one of the latest mysteries recommended by SRL. This you will read and return within two weeks. On each alternate Thursday after you receive the first book, you will apply at the same place, within the same hours, to the same person, and in the same manner; and you will receive another book, which you will return promptly in two weeks.

Within three days after the receipt of this communication, you will deliver two unmarked dollar bills in a sealed envelope to the above person at the above place, as a token of your bond for the term of six months to the conspiracy known as The Campus Crime Club.

I have the honor, *mon cher monsieur,* to subscribe myself, with distinguished compliments,

Yours for more baffling mysteries,

SERGEANT CUFF

Every one of my chosen eleven appeared promptly at the book shop, and the "proprietress" was amused to have dignified professors bending down to whisper in her ear, "I am Ebenezer Gryce," or "I am Lord Peter Wimsey," or *"Je m'apelle Hercule Poirot."* During the life of the Campus Crime Club, many curious incidents developed, most of them resulting from efforts of the members to "detect" the anonymities involved. But before the end of the second six-months' term, the secret mumbo-jumbo had worn thin; and we concluded the whole project with an "unveiling dinner"—at which I discovered that one man (with whom I was not at the time on speaking terms) had got himself into the group quite unknown to me!

This was fun. Mystery romances are reading fun for millions these days—high-, middle-, and low-brow. We are not disturbed when a critic like Edmund Wilson declares in the *New Yorker* that he has not read a good detective story since Sherlock Holmes. On the other hand, most of us will not go as far as Somerset Maugham did in a *Saturday Evening Post* article when he wrote: "It may well be that posterity, turning a cold shoulder to the more pretentious efforts of our day, will acclaim the crime story as the most characteristic and remarkable feature of English literature in the twentieth century."

The critics may say their say, but we go on reading our favorite mystery writers. To many of us it seems

obvious that the great trouble with contemporary detective stories is not that they are escapist literature or
that they do not concern themselves enough with social
and political problems, but that too many of them are
ill conceived and ill written.   One must walk warily
among them, choosing with care.

Escapism?   That is a scarecrow word.   It does not
frighten confirmed readers of such literature.   We know
that escape from the grind of daily tasks and personal
anxieties is often therapeutic or (not to be pseudo-
scientific about it) just plain restful and relaxing.   To be
sure, good things are liable to abuse, and one must not
do too much "ostriching."   No normal reader wants a
steady diet of detective stories.

A few years ago, in a book about best sellers, I wrote
a little essay that led to the not very original conclusion
that "all general reading is escapism."   Since then I have
come across an observation in an old volume of Sir
Arthur Helps's *Friends in Council:* "Reading is sometimes
an ingenious device for avoiding thought."   And the other
day Malcolm Muggeridge wryly remarked that print has
tended to drive out thought, and now the electronic
screen threatens to drive out print.   All of which has
some validity; but such talk rather obscures the central
truth of the matter, which is that a varied regimen of
reading opens windows on all sides, helps to orient the
reader in the universe, and in turn instructs, delights,
stimulates, and amuses us.

Variety is of the essence in a good reading program.
Like others of our tribe, I like to have three or four books
on hand at a time—a new biography, for example, a
thoughtful treatise on some contemporary problem, a
fresh and readable book of essays or reminiscence, some
old-new favorite, and a good mystery.   Or what have you.

Perhaps a new or old book of verse, or a novel that everybody says we should read. Of course, not all of these books deserve equal attention. We are all familiar with the wise Baconian distinctions between books to be tasted, to be swallowed, and to be chewed and digested. But some books are ruined by too much chewing. I myself am no longer a "heavy" reader, always searching for symbols, sources, parallels, and such. I have had my turn at that game, but in these later years I prefer to read for what the writer seems to offer to the fairly intelligent adult.

My wife and I still read aloud a little every day. As in other things, enjoyment shared is doubled. And we like to own most of the books we read, even though that means disposing of some that have served their purpose to make room for newcomers on overcrowded shelves.

We inveterate readers can all stand up with Edward Gibbon and repeat after him the testimony that he gave when he was an old man writing his *Memoirs,* on what he owed to his "early and invincible love of reading, which I would not exchange for all the treasures of India." It is indeed a *love* of reading that we mean—a passion for books. That is why I have chosen to entitle this essay "An Amateur Reader," using the adjective in its old, etymological sense of "lover." It has been a love, for better or worse, throughout life.

5

Chautauqua

ON THE SHORE OF CHARMING Lake Chautauqua, in the southwestern corner of the state of New York, is a wooded area in which the Methodists held seasonal camp meetings during the years shortly after the Civil War. But by the mid-seventies, those old shouting and praying outdoor "revivals" under canvas were dying out; and the Lake Chautauqua grounds were taken over in 1874 for something new in the world—a Sunday school Assembly.

John H. Vincent, later a Methodist bishop, was at this time engaged in working out a system for the training of Sunday school teachers; and Lewis Miller, a wealthy and religious manufacturer, was his enthusiastic supporter. These two were the founders of what came to be known as "Chautauqua." The first Assembly, designed to impart biblical lore and religious teaching to those who came to the lakeside to camp for two or three weeks, was a great success; and the number of patrons grew rapidly year by year. Soon the Assembly had outgrown the bounds of its original pattern—in scope of study, in entertainment features, in length of program, in equipment. An amphitheater was erected; good dining rooms were provided; small frame hotels offered accommodations for those who did not wish to live in canvas dwellings during the sessions.

But the great development was in the breadth of the program, which burst sectarian bounds almost from the start and soon became thoroughly interdenominational. Sunday school work, though not abandoned, was soon overshadowed by courses in secular history and literature. William Rainey Harper, later to become the first president of the University of Chicago, was brought in to direct the cultural courses. Vincent, a promoter of genius, induced President Grant to visit the Assembly and address it in 1875. That gave the institution on the shore of Lake Chautauqua a national standing, and it also made it easier to get men like General Garfield, Schuyler Colfax, and President Hayes in later seasons. And hundreds of famous preachers, authors, and educators were proud to be invited to speak at Chautauqua in the eighties and nineties.

The spectacular success of the Assembly on the lake with the romantic Indian name led to imitation; and soon other institutes of the kind were being established all over the country, all calling themselves "Chautauquas." Each of them had its barn-like "pavilion," or auditorium, its cottages, its tents, its rude classrooms, and its inn or dining room. And each, of course, had its own program of lectures by famous men and women, its concerts and entertainments, its courses of study, and so on.

But an even greater expansion of this adult education project in a different direction followed. It was in the fourth year of the Chautauqua Assembly that Vincent promulgated an idea designed to spread the blessings of higher education far and wide. He himself had not been able to attend college as a young man, and he felt a keen sympathy for all who had been denied that opportunity.

What he now proposed was a four-year home-reading course dealing with the chief civilizations of the world. His first list included seven very solid books, and the prescribed work ended with examinations and what was called "recognition" for those who passed. This new system was called the Chautauqua Literary and Scientific Circle, and it soon became immensely successful. By the end of the century some fifty thousand men and women had been "recognized" for their completion of the four-year course, and a quarter of a million had been enrolled for some period, long or short. A new reading list, with books in special binding, was provided each year. History, literature, sociology, and science courses furnished the chief materials for the studies outlined during some fifty years; and the great civilizations of mankind were covered by those courses.

When I was a young boy in Tipton, Iowa, I was charmed and fascinated by that exciting thing which we knew as "Chautauqua." My parents were among the organizers of the Tipton Circle; and every Monday night they would depart for the meeting, each carrying a C.L.&S.C. book or two and a folding chair. Since the meetings were in private homes, members saved hosts the trouble of borrowing chairs from the neighbors by bringing their own. To me there was something enchanting about those folding chairs, which were kept upstairs in the spare room except when Father and Mother carried them off on Monday nights. Once when our parents left us alone in the house to attend a funeral out in the country, we fetched those folding chairs downstairs and set them up in the sitting room, intending to replace them long before Father and Mother got back. But their return was unexpectedly early, and I was sitting in one of the magical contraptions when they walked into the house.

"Why, how did this chair ever get down here?" asked Mother.

"I brought it down, Mamma," I confessed.

"But why did thee bring it down here?"

"I don't know, Mamma."

"Well, thee can just take it right back upstairs, and the other one, too!"

Mamma did not know the reason those chairs fascinated me, and Frankie did not know, and I am not sure that I can explain it satisfactorily at this late date; but I think that our parents' enthusiasm for Chautauqua had been communicated to us and that we felt a kind of sorcery in everything connected with it. Thus the folding chair was a true fetish. But even if we were forbidden to handle the folding chairs, we were allowed to read the books and the *Chautauquan,* the Circle's excellent monthly magazine. Some of the books were beyond our capacities; indeed, I suppose all of them were, but I remember with affection Henry A. Beers's *Initial Studies in American Letters,* and I recall puzzling over W. C. Brownell's *French Traits.* Also we had a "Chautauqua Desk," which was a combined blackboard- and wall-desk with a revolving scroll at the top, and which afforded us endless delight and instruction.

Many years later, Chautauqua again affected my life significantly, through a new development of the old system that Vincent and his colleagues had originated in the seventies. I have pointed out how hundreds of Assemblies had sprung up throughout the land, each with its own plot of ground and rude buildings, and how each was offering a program for both visitors and campers. Toward the end of the nineties, many Chautauquas were depending more upon season-ticket holders from their own communities than upon campers. Though these Assemblies were all the progeny of the pioneer venture on Lake Chautauqua, the management there never made any attempt to organize them into one interdependent system. The common need for inspirational and instructive speakers and good concert companies did, however, produce a certain amount of co-operative effort in program building; and soon the lyceum agencies, which furnished talent to lecture courses the country over in the winters, began to serve these summer programs also, thus giving their speakers and musicians work in both seasons.

Then, just after the turn of the century, it occurred to several men in the lyceum business that many more towns could be served far more cheaply if the agency furnished not only the talent but also tent auditoriums, as the circus did; in such a system they would ask local help only to sponsor the Chautauqua by guaranteeing the sale of a certain number of season tickets, as was done in connection with the winter lecture courses. Such an arrangement could keep talent busy every day of the season, reduce "jumps" on the average from five hundred to fifty miles, and enable a town to have a full week's cultural debauch without any permanent investment or any exertion beyond that of ticket-selling campaigns. Leader in this momentous shift of emphasis in the Chautauqua system was Keith Vawter, of Cedar Rapids, Iowa, a lyceum operator who founded the tent circuit named after him in 1904. Ten or fifteen years later, when the tent Chautauqua reached its height, over seven thousand towns were being served by circuits operated by a score or more of agencies.

Urban critics sometimes satirized the tent Chautauqua. They made fun of Bryan and La Follette and

Champ Clark for "hitting the Chautauqua trail" every summer; but the good old *Baltimore Sun* was right when, in discussing Secretary of State Bryan's speaking tour of the summer of 1914, it declared that no prominent public official could afford to neglect the Chautauqua platform. Certainly many of them spent a few weeks in such work each season for a number of years. Senator Harding, of Ohio, was a familiar figure at the Chautauquas, as were Senator Lenroot, of Wisconsin; Senator Norris, of Nebraska; Governor Folk, of Missouri; and "Uncle Joe" Cannon, of Illinois. Among headliners were Judge Lindsey, of Colorado, on the youth question, and Captain Richmond P. Hobson, a war hero, on military and naval preparedness. Audiences were made to forget the heat and hard benches by such humorists as Strickland Gillilan, Opie Read, and James Whitcomb Riley. Choirs, orchestras, bands, string quartets, vocal quartets, bellringers, interpretive readers, chalk-talkers, violinists, and pianists furnished rich variety. Every good program had at least one dramatic company, offering a full-length play.

Talent's lot was not easy. Nightly "jumps," often on the inferior trains that served the small towns; daily appearances, excused only in cases of serious illness; all kinds of weather, including torrid midsummer heat, rain beating on tent tops, wind that often made the quarter-poles dance a frightening jig, country hotels and irregular meals—such were the hardships of the Chautauqua troupers. But season tickets had been sold on the basis of an advertised program; the show had to go on.

I remember one blistering hot afternoon in a small Iowa town when Bryan was on the platform, and the orator was drenched with perspiration. He stopped in the middle of one of his rounded periods, dipped both hands into a large pitcher of ice water that stood on the table before him, and came up with two handfuls of crushed ice, which he held to his throbbing bald head for a minute or two. There was no laughter; we all felt sympathetic towards the old man.

One season Congressman Victor Murdock, of Kansas, an excellent platform man, suffered for a couple of weeks with what we called "summer complaint." His lecture was an hour and a quarter long; and one afternoon, finding it impossible to postpone relief until his address was over, he stopped suddenly in the midst of a sentence and said: "Friends, this is a hot afternoon, and I must not keep you sitting on those hard planks for another half-hour without change of position. I am going to give you five minutes' intermission so you can stand up and stretch your legs." The audience was surprised and pleased by the speaker's thoughtfulness; but before it had "stretched its legs" very much, Vic had slipped through the curtains at the back of the platform, had made a bee-line for the barbed wire fence that separated the Chautauqua lot from a nearby cornfield, and was out of sight of even the tent-boys among the green stalks of the growing corn. When the five-minute intermission was over, the speaker was back on the platform, composed and relieved, and ready to continue his vigorous and entertaining lecture. Such was the life of a follower of the Chautauqua trail.

In the summer of 1916, when I was editing and publishing a weekly paper in Grand Junction, Iowa, I added to my various business, civic, and church responsibilities the duties of local manager of the town's Chautauqua. In fact, I not only performed the duties of that functionary but also acted as platform manager for the Grand Junction program that year. The next spring, having sold my newspaper in order to begin graduate work at Columbia University the next fall, I was ready to accept

Sam Holladay's offer of a summer job as a platform manager on Circuit A of his Midland Chautauqua System. I
liked the work so well on first trial that I returned to it
for the three succeeding summers.

This Circuit A had seven Chautauqua programs running at once, a new one beginning every day. There
were eight tents and eight crews in order to allow a day
between set-ups to transport and erect the tent and get
ready for a new opening. The crew was composed of the
platform manager, who was really a general superintendent; two tent-boys, usually college students on "vacation," who had the care of the big tent and the canvas
yard-walls and lived in a small utility tent on the grounds;
and the junior supervisor, who conducted the morning
play hours for the children and usually trained them for
a "pageant" that was staged the last day of the session.

The first thing the platform manager had to do on
arriving in a new town was to look up the local manager
and learn how the season ticket sale had gone. The
entire circuit Chautauqua system was built on the season
ticket. No town was served by the Midland without a
contract guaranteeing the sale of a thousand dollars'
worth of season tickets, signed by a group of public-
spirited men. Alas, the sale sometimes fell short, and in
such a case the local manager was naturally inclined to
avoid the unpleasant business of collecting the guarantee
from his neighbors, and the platform man had to take up
that task. More than once I had to make the rounds
collecting the guarantee and then to follow up those visits
with a campaign to enlist signers for the next year's contract. That, gentle reader, was what is known as a
Herculean task. Sometimes I succeeded, and sometimes
I had to give it up and mark the town off the list. The
Bureau sent out a clean-up man to help with business

affairs on the last day, but I usually had the contract all signed up for him or else was ready with conclusive evidence that the place was no longer what we called "a good Chautauqua town."

The public knew the platform manager chiefly as the fellow who introduced the talent. A short and sharp introduction, including a wisecrack or two and a flattering resumé of the record and reputation of the speaker or artist, was called for. Sometimes the speaker, who loved the flattery, would use it to serve the double purpose of a pretense of modesty and a laugh-provoker with which to begin an otherwise rather heavy address. I remember a certain famous New York pulpit orator who fell into the habit of quipping about my introductions and (as I heard from the grapevine circuit) about those of all the other platform managers. One afternoon, after I had introduced this speaker in my best manner, and the greeting applause had subsided, he looked over to the wings into which I had disappeared from audience view and asked, "Why hasn't somebody shot that fellow in the leg before this?" After the lecture, I waylaid the great man, who was at the time in company with a Bureau representative, and though I did not shoot him in the leg, I fired a barrage of rebuke and objurgation at him point-blank. He seemed genuinely surprised that I had been offended, and was so apologetic that he almost wept. He had regarded the banter, I found, as part of his show, and had not stopped to think that the platform man had to live with the people of a town, and deal with them, throughout a week, and needed to perserve some modicum of respect and standing. That was my first season, and I suppose I was too sensitive.

The platform manager had to be a kind of guide and shepherd to the talent. I met them on the arrival of their trains whenever I could. I gave them advice about hotels, eating places, travel arrangements, location of the tent, how to please local audiences, cures for headache and stomach-ache, how to get along with their traveling companions, what to write to the family at home, and a hundred other things. Relaxed somewhere after the evening program, a speaker or musician would amaze me by taking me into his confidence about his marital difficulties, or troubles he was having with his publisher, or his anxieties about his lyceum contract, or the exciting details of his recent surgical operation.

I had some odd characters on my platform during the four summers in which I was engaged in this work, including some who were phonies, some who were too temperamental to endure patiently the rigors of the circuit Chautauqua, some who were everlastingly flirtatious, and some who never did find out exactly what it was all about.

I remember one lecturer on big-game hunting who began his summer's work by devoting his hour mainly to a great lion hunt in which he had engaged. He did not last out our season; but before he was replaced, he had built up his story to where he was slaughtering half the wild life of the South African veldts singlehandedly. That sort of accretion of sensation was easy for a speaker who was naturally a fluent liar and was daily subjected to the challenge of a thrill-hungry audience. On the 1917 program we had a male quartet made up of disabled Canadian soldiers returned from the European war. They sang the songs then becoming popular—"Tipperary," "The Long, Long Trail," "Over There"—and did them very well; and in between, one of them told something of their experiences in the war. This narrative contained, at the very first, something about the crimes committed by the "Huns"; and as the season progressed, these atrocity stories grew. Since I listened to the program every week, I could see this development clearly and was shocked by what appeared to be a singularly repulsive variety of mendacity. So I complained to the Bureau, and soon the boys mended their ways and cleaned up their story and sang "Over There" with more verve than ever, and less sadism.

One of the most temperamental lecturers I had on my platform was an English lieutenant, also a war hero. In his voluminous luggage he carried a hammock, because, he insisted, he could not sleep in hotel beds. He had an injured knee and walked with a cane, so his traveling companions had to assist him with his luggage; and they came to resent that hammock so much that several times they tried to lose it by forgetting to bring it off the train, but the lieutenant always recovered it. If he had come to us from His Majesty's Navy, we might have understood this peculiarity; but he came from the army. Every night he would swing that hammock, usually in his hotel room, but sometimes outdoors.

The lieutenant was always full of complaints about the way the Chautauqua was run, and I regret to record that I quarreled with him almost continuously the whole season long. He may have been suffering all the time from his wounds, though I thought then it was sheer ill temper. He had a rough, unpleasant voice, a fine sense of his own importance, a very British manner of speech, and a monocle. The last of these appurtenances he used but rarely, bringing it out only to emphasize some particularly insulting observation. One night in Mankato, Kansas, when our tent had blown down and we had to give our show in the open, the lieutenant refused until the last minute to go on. Speaking without benefit of canvas would hurt his voice, he argued. I threatened him with all the condign discipline I could conjure up in the name of the Bureau, but I was not sure until I had actually introduced him and he limped forward from the front row of the audience that he would speak that night.

The "leftenant" was supposed to be writing a book about his American experiences, and he once told me that I would be surprised to know what he had in his notes about me. I do not know whether or not he ever published his book or whether I was in it if he did; but here he is in mine, complete with hammock, limp, and monocle.

But there were many great troupers on the old Midland Circuit A, and some really distinguished personalities. With some of the talent I made lasting friendships, and I looked forward to my weekly reunions with them in happy anticipation of little parties and much good talk. Strickland Gillilan, the humorist-author of the famous "Off ag'in, on ag'in, gone ag'in, Finnegin" verses—was a rare soul and a good companion. Chancellor Buchtel, of Denver University, former Governor of Colorado and one of our top lecturers, virtually adopted me as a grandson for a season. Governor Leslie M. Shaw, of Iowa, was an inexhaustible treasury of homely wisdom. Theodore Roosevelt had appointed him secretary of the treasury partly, it was said, because of the national reputation as a campaign speaker that he had made when he had spoken from hundreds of platforms in the canvass of 1900; but I noticed that he was always nervous before he went on for his Chautauqua lecture. One evening when I saw him pacing back and forth behind the curtain, I bantered him a little about his obvious tenseness.

"Governor," I said, "I should think that a seasoned stump-speaker like you would take this sort of thing in stride—just one more talk to an audience, you know. But here you are, nervous as a kitten!"

"My boy," said the Governor, "you talk like a tyro, as you are. No man ever yet made a speech that was worth hearing without getting wound up tight enough to bust a spring before he went on. Remember that."

I have indeed remembered that. I accepted it then, and I accept it now, as basic in the psychology of address.

Occasionally I had William Jennings Bryan on my platform. His fee was always half his gate receipts. I never got through to him personally; he was kind to Chautauqua personnel but uninterested. It was once necessary for me to travel about fifty miles in an automobile with him, and that was in the days when such a trip required nearly two hours. I had looked forward to listening to some personal words of wit and wisdom from the great man on this occasion, but he was apparently saving them for his audience at two bits a head, for as soon as he settled himself in his seat and we got under way, his head drooped and he was asleep. All I heard from him on the whole journey was an occasional gurgling snore. Like a good trouper, he was getting his rest where he could.

Memories of my Chautauqua summers are compounded chiefly of meetings with interesting people, campaigns for contracts, and weather. Weather was a constant hazard. Windstorms were especially to be feared. Sizzling heat under the big top, light showers and drumming rains we could cope with, but high winds might do great damage to tents and were sometimes a potential danger to the lives and limbs of audiences. The worst experience of that kind that ever came my way was the baby cyclone at Mankato, Kansas.

We came to Mankato that year doomed to misfortune.

Kansas had been suffering from a summer-long drought, the fields were dead, and neither farmers nor towns-people had money for Chautauqua. The town had not met its contract guarantee, and we had only small audiences at our programs. One afternoon, a blessed black cloud appeared in the west, and ahead of it moved white wind-puffs. The talent were alarmed; but I told them to go on when introduced, and I would warn them in time if there was danger. Then, as I watched the cloud, I saw it part, half going north of us and half south, leaving Mankato as parched and dry as it had been all summer. The next day Dr. Lena K. Sadler was on the platform delivering her excellent health lecture when the same thing happened: the menacing bank of clouds came out of the west, with wind in front of it. But this time it did not part; the black wall seemed to rush straight toward our tent, and the wind was upon us.

I bounced onto the platform and asked the audience to get out. "It is my duty," I cried, "to warn you that this tent will not be safe in five minutes! We'll give you the rest of this program later if we can, but for now you must find shelter somewhere else!" But the small audience was not much alarmed by the antics of the frightened young fellow on the platform. The tall Kansan who was our local manager rose in the rear of the tent and drawled, "Oh, we're used to these winds here in Kansas, Mr. Mott. We're not afraid of them. We'd love to have a little blow and a big rain!" But I argued that nobody would be safe in that tent when the wind lifted the quarter-poles; and nearly all of the audience drifted out, more amused than alarmed.

The tent-boys had, of course, begun to tighten guy ropes and tie down the canvas walls. In a few minutes the wind was whistling under the top, making it billow and pull on the ropes. The quarter-poles were attached to the canvas; and when the top rose they went with it and then came crashing down upon seats and benches and everything beneath them. This infernal dance of the quarter-poles was now accompanied by the roaring of the wind, the tearing of the canvas, and the perilous swaying of the big center-poles. Suddenly one of these poles cracked with a noise like artillery, and the big tent came down.

Nobody was hurt. The wind and the rain were soon past. But the tent was ruined, and that night we gave our show under the stars. We had the largest crowd of our Mankato week that night. For the remaining two days of our session, we held forth in the high-school assembly hall, which was large enough for our audiences, with space to spare. But we could not collect our guarantee in Mankato; we failed to get a contract for the next year; and after the last program, when the borrowed piano was being returned to its owner, it slid off the back of the dray and lost most of its imitation mahogany case in the ditch. Thus ended a week of disasters.

I recall a more amusing experience with a storm in Waseca, Minnesota. There the tent was pitched in the public park; and since the space between the trees was a little cramped for a tent, the boys had tied their guy ropes to trees in many cases and had not been able to get an evenly stretched top. However, it did well enough until a thunderstorm came along one afternoon with a few puffs of wind before it. These made the canvas billow and flap more than it would have done with a tight set-up. I had been watching the clouds and took the responsibility of telling the audience there was no danger and they had better remain in the tent, where it was dry, instead of rushing out into the rain. They agreed, but it was a different story with the talent. We had a ladies' orchestra with a male director on the platform that afternoon, and the Major had, I believe, undergone some harrowing experiences with a wind-wrecked tent in a former season; at any rate, he shouted a *sauve qui peut* to his girls, and he himself, a big round man, dived under the platform, trying to drag his big round bass drum with him. It took half an hour to restore order and set the harmonies and rhythms of the orchestra to competing with the beat of the rain on the canvas roof.

But on the whole, my four Chautauqua summers were pleasant and rewarding. The emotional galvanism characteristic of all show business, the weekly change of scene, and the constant association with lively-minded people combined to create a rich experience for me.

Now the Chautauqua circuits are all gone, and of course the Chautauqua Literary and Scientific Circle dropped into oblivion years ago. All that is left of the grand old institution of Chautauqua is a small, scattered group of die-hard independent Assemblies, mostly occupying their own "pavilions" and situated in various resort areas—and the mother of them all, at Lake Chautauqua. That great institution now flourishes more grandly than ever, retaining still its fine buildings and elaborate programs, on the shore of the beautiful lake with the Indian name.

6

Profiles of Professors

WHAT IS A COLLEGE? Buildings, of course, more or less adequate; laboratories and libraries, also more or less adequate. A campus, which may be mere pavement to traverse in passing from one class to another, or a beautiful greensward shaded by trees and bordered by river or lake. But these are facilities and backgrounds; the real meaning of a college lies in the faculty and student body and what they do.

Well, what do they do? They lecture and they study; they pursue a complicated maze involving curricula, examinations, grades, promotions; they organize furiously, into social clubs, cultural societies, committees and committees and committees; they produce exhibitions of football, basketball, and baseball, as well as concerts, plays, and debates. They publish newspapers and magazines; they indulge in bull sessions without end.

These activities are "college." They are evolved in a faculty-student relationship, and their value depends much upon the quality of the faculty and the capacity of the student body. It is inescapable: the essence of a college education is always a Mark Hopkins on one end of a log and a young Garfield on the other. It was so in primitive times, it was so in my own youth, it is so today.

No Garfield I; but I was an eager student, and I had some memorable teachers.

The faculty of Simpson College, when I was a student there shortly after the turn of the century, was not a really distinguished group. That is to say, none of them had a national reputation as scholar, writer, or educational leader. The president was the only one listed in *Who's Who in America*. And yet some of them were great personalities. It is better to be enshrined in the memories of generations of students than in the pages of *Who's Who*.

"Prexy" Shelton was a handsome figure of a man with a grey, professorial Vandyke beard. That beard apparently tickled his face a little, for he was wont to rub it absent-mindedly as he stood before us in chapel admonishing us earnestly, yet half-humorously, not to make paths across the green carpet which lay under the "whispering maples" of the campus. Charles Eldred Shelton was a born platform man, much in demand as a speaker on notable occasions and even as a special pleader for the college, but disappointing in the classroom. I took a course in English history under him and found that he relied largely on class recitations from a textbook and assigned readings in the historical fiction of Bulwer, Scott, and others. I think teaching must have been a chore to him, but in chapel he was a great figure; his language had a richness of style and allusion which always held and sometimes fascinated us.

The Reverend W. E. Hamilton, D.D., occupied the Buxton chair of moral and intellectual philosophy, and the respect which he was shown in the community was almost reverential. His was a short, stocky figure, clad in the black cloth of his profession, with coat to the knees, whether he was in the pulpit or at the classroom desk.

His hair and his beard (which he wore full except for a shaven upper lip) were white and impressive. His voice was clear and his eyes sometimes seemed to look straight into one's very soul. I have to confess that I sometimes found his lectures dull, though they always sounded profound. I took the required course in "Bible" under him and also one in civics. In the latter course his textbook was Francis Lieber's *Manual of Political Ethics*, which had been first published in the 1830's; though rather out of date, it was a good solid work.

The session of Doctor Hamilton's class I remember best was one in which he used almost the entire period to inveigh against the offense of certain students who, the night before, had plastered sidewalks and walls about the campus with a "proc." Perhaps few readers of these pages will recall what the old class proclamations were like: they are now happily forgotten. A "proc" was in the form of a circus poster, printed in three colors, advertising a group of monstrosities soon to be exhibited. But each of these freaks was easily recognizable as a member of the rival class, or even of the faculty; indeed, names were freely used. It was all very libelous, was necessarily printed out of town, and was posted prominently in the dead of night. Once alerted, authorities became very busy removing the offensive things in the early hours of the morning, but nearly everyone usually had a chance to see at least one copy. Well, that morning Doctor Hamilton discoursed on the crime of libel, the sin of anonymity, the sadistic cruelty implicit in giving pain to the innocent, and so on. All the time, it seemed to me, he was looking straight at me, and through me, and into the secrets of my black heart. For I was the guilty youth. To be sure, I had a co-conspirator whom I shall not name now out of respect for the high position that he has long held. I dare say he is today as ashamed of our midnight deed as I am, and that he can declare, as I can, that he has never since made an anonymous attack on anyone or anything.

The Simpson College teacher from whom I received the most intellectual stimulation was Martha Stahl, professor of Latin. She not only introduced us to the ideas of the Ciceronian essays, the charms of Horace, and the comedies of Plautus, but also she made us correlate the Roman civilization with our own. Miss Stahl was a woman of strong frame; she wore high-necked shirtwaists (as they were called) and long, heavy skirts. She had a high forehead, level grey eyes, and a firm mouth. She liked to talk to her class about the social and political problems of the day; and I am afraid that sometimes when we were unprepared to recite our lines from Horace, we led her to comment at length on some topic that had been suggested in that morning's leading editorial in the *Des Moines Register*. I took courses with Miss Stahl throughout all my years at Simpson, and found her a never-failing source of inspiration.

John L. Tilton was professor of natural sciences. He was a brisk man with a large mustache and a passion for geology. Once when he was for a short time acting president of the college, he revised the curriculum to make geology a required subject for every student in every department. After all, were not all subjects, and all life and all civilization indeed, based on the fundament of the structure of the earth itself? Doctor Tilton was a New Englander, and his down-east speech was odd in midwestern ears. When geology students trained by him took graduate work at the universities of our region, they were always recognized as Simpson graduates because when they talked about the Iowa loess, they called it "lurss."

Chief representative of European culture among us was Frank E. Barrows, director of the Conservatory of Music. He had studied in Berlin, he visited Paris often, and the walls of his home (open only to a favored few) were literally covered with paintings he had picked up abroad. He encouraged his favorite students, such as John J. Landsbury and Everett Olive, to study abroad. Perhaps his most famous graduate was Arthur D. Middleton, who eventually became a Metropolitan Opera baritone. Big "Mid's" magnificent voice was the pride of the college, especially when he sang the "Toreador" song. The conservatory was then a very important part of Simpson. I was happy when I somehow managed to pass a test and was permitted to sing in the "Hallelulia Chorus" at Christmas time, and I still value my early friendship with Olive and Landsbury.

I left Simpson at the end of my third year. I left without a degree mainly because the University of Chicago was then offering a fourth undergraduate year in which the liberal arts were combined with beginning courses in law, and I had suddenly decided to become a lawyer. My flirtation with the law did not last long, however. With each class in torts, criminal law, or contracts, the realization grew upon me that the practice of the law was essentially altercation, and that I did not want to dedicate my life to contentiousness. I have since learned, of course, that all life is contention; but I still have the feeling that lawyers (or many of them) feed upon quarrels and dissension. My aversion is probably due to my family tradition of quietism: I never knew a Quaker to go to law.

Then there was the matter of odors. Sitting in my law

classes at the University, listening to my fellows recite
and the professors lecture, I breathed in (especially when
the wind was in the right direction) the strong, over-
mastering stench of the stockyards. I could scarcely
blame the complications of contract law for this, but my
growing distaste for legal subtleties came to be identified
unreasonably with the stockyard smell. On the other
hand, every day, as I passed by the open windows of the
University Press going to and from classes, I caught the
whiff of freshly printed sheets. Ah, the ineffable odor
of printing ink on paper just from the presses! Araby
has no perfume like it. So I accepted my father's offer to
go into partnership with him and buy a newspaper and
printing plant. Thus are life's decisions sometimes made.

The greatest teacher I encountered at the University
of Chicago was Edward Scribner Ames. His "Introduction to Philosophy" affected me more profoundly than
any other course I ever pursued in my undergraduate
years. But closely related to my first knowledge of the
Greek philosophers was the revolution in my thinking in
theology that resulted from a regular Sunday attendance
at the little church just off the campus at which Ames
preached. In these two classrooms I was freed from many
fears and superstitions and given a new set of ideas to
work on. I knew at that time how Christian, in Bunyan's
allegory, felt when he was relieved of his great burden
and given fresh garments in which to pursue his journey.
Perhaps I overstate the matter; but Ames, who had been
a center of controversy in his own church and who at the
time I knew him held a university rank no higher than
that of instructor, opened liberating gates for my mind
and spirit.

The big word with Doctor Ames was "empiricism."
Rooted in the philosophy of John Locke, growing through

John Stuart Mill and others, this way of thinking came to its American flowering, I suppose, in William James, whose fine passages Ames loved to quote, and John Dewey, with whom Ames worked at Chicago. For Ames, who was well grounded in psychology, religion was itself empirical, proving itself in practice; the figure of Jesus was empirical and thus stripped of what are sometimes called "supernatural" elements; and even the idea of God was empirical. I was fascinated by the study of popular ideas of God. Riding on the elevated, I used to engage my seat-mate in conversation only to lead slyly up to the inquiry, "What do you think God is?" I received some curious answers, but I noticed that most of my guinea pigs seemed to think I was some kind of crank (as I dare say I was), and so I eventually gave up my "survey." I came to think of God as whatever highest ideals and aims an individual may conceive of, admire, reverence, and serve. This was not, to be sure, quite Ames's concept, but I hope and believe that he would not have been wholly displeased with it. Friends have sometimes told me that such a faith is "atheistic," but I am reminded of that wry observation once made by J. H. Randall, the Columbia philosopher, that belief in the existence of God is at least one form of atheism from which he is free.

I have long been fascinated by the old-fashioned theological phrase, "state of grace." For me it has meant an inner sense of my own integrity—and I use that word in its larger meaning. I confess that I have not always enjoyed such a "state of grace," but I have always reached for it.

Perhaps I should not say, as I have, that I ever "knew" Doctor Ames. To me he was a teacher on a rostrum or in a pulpit. Unpretentious, without mannerisms or eccentricities in appearance or speech, he was gifted with

great lucidity of language and forthrightness of presentation. I once called upon him in his office, which I
found tucked away in a carrel of the divinity library. I
wished only to tell him how much his course had meant
to me. I think he was a little puzzled at first by my
awkward words, and then a little pleased; but I soon left
him to his studies.

This incident leads me to record here my conviction
that much of the talk about the necessity of fraternization
between faculty and students is exaggerated and affected.
In a seminar or small class or in advisement on a thesis,
a close relationship is natural; but a great teacher ought
not to have to impose his personality upon his students
like a candidate running for office. I did not respect
Edward Scribner Ames the less for his dignity and reserve.

Another teacher at Chicago whom I remember with
pleasure was Floyd R. Mechem, the scholarly gentleman
with grey Vandyke and gentle voice who effortlessly held
in check our large and rather turbulent class in torts. His
specialty, I believe, was the law of agency, but he managed to impart to this group of freshman law students
a respect for the logic and the historical development of
the common law.

Some years later, when I was picking up some summer
credits at the State University of Iowa for transfer to
Columbia, I sat in the classes of two great teachers of
English—Hardin Craig and Thomas A. Knott. The
former, a well-known scholar in Renaissance and Eliza-
bethan literature, has probably brought an appreciation
of Shakespeare to the minds of more college students
than any other man alive. I knew him well when I became a member of his English faculty at Iowa in the
1920's, and owed much to his helpful guidance. Tommy
Knott, Chaucerian and philologist, was a fine example of

the sound scholar with a tough core of common sense. To hear him talk, in his informal way, on almost any subject was to acquire, by intellectual osmosis, a scholarly temper. Square-jawed, with humorous, sharp eyes, always lighting his corncob pipe with the kitchen matches he carried about with him, he was an inveterate encourager of younger scholars. Iowa lost him when the Merriams took him east to Springfield, Massachusetts, to edit the second edition of *Webster's New International Dictionary.*

During my earlier work at Columbia University, I was much under the influence of George Philip Krapp. In my experience he was a new professorial type. A bit dandified, with his mustache, bright ties, and walking-stick, he was friendly and stimulating. He was a teacher in the Socratic tradition and a linguistic investigator who immediately set his students to work collecting speech phenomena within their own experience. His tireless devotion to such researches inspired me with the fascination of the study of words and usages. My master's thesis was a collectanea of Iowa pioneer speech, and there was a time when I thought American philology would be my area of specialization; but as it turned out, I have been only an interested (and always fascinated) spectator on the sidelines of that scholarly field. But Professor Krapp I have always remembered, with gratitude for his personal helpfulness and with admiration for his wide interests and diversified literary talents.

Such diversity was characteristic of other figures on the Columbia campus as well. Brander Matthews was serving his last few years as professor of dramatic literature when I was there. His students all called him affectionately by his first nàme when they spoke of him among themselves. None of them will forget his somewhat stooped figure at his lecture desk; his short, scraggly beard, grey except where it was yellowed about the mouth by the cigarettes that he smoked constantly; his interesting lectures, filled with anecdotes of the many famous literary and theatrical figures he had known. I remember his use of the word "anecdotage," a coinage that he ascribed, I think, to "Dizzy, first Earl of Beaconsfield," but applied to himself. When I came up at last for my doctoral examination, "Brander" was in retirement; but he did me the honor to return to the campus to hear me defend my dissertation. It was not I, however, but my subject that brought him to that meeting, I think; I had written on the history of the American magazines of the 1870's, all of which he had seen and in which he had once played a part. When the old *Galaxy* was mentioned, he remarked that his first published essay had appeared in that magazine. This I knew very well, and could have reminded him of its title, but did not. Here was a stooped, grey-bearded ancient: could I remind him that his entry into the world of letters had been made by an essay on "The Art of Kissing"?

Carl Van Doren was another Columbia teacher whom I thoroughly enjoyed. He was headmaster of Brearley School downtown, and came up to the campus once a week to lecture for two hours on contemporary American literature. He had a big class. He would stand before it, a stalwart figure with close-cropped hair and quite without professorial affectations, and begin talking in a conversational tone without any notes; at the end of fifty minutes of uninterrupted discourse, he would stop and announce a ten-minute recess. The ten minutes up, he would begin again and continue uninterruptedly for fifty minutes more. He had read everything, it seemed, and knew all of the important authors and publishers and all of the literary currents and trends.

I owed much, then and later, to Carl Van Doren; and it is a joy to me to think that eventually I made some slight repayment in kind to him. I treasure a note that he wrote to me when he was in the midst of the preparation of his masterpiece of biography, the life of Benjamin Franklin. Chester A. Jorgenson, a colleague of mine at Iowa, had collaborated with me in making up a book of selections from Franklin's writings, for which we supplied notes and an introduction of 188 pages. On April 1, 1937, my former teacher took time off from his labors to type a laudatory note to me about the "Mott and Jorgenson Franklin" which closed with the sentence: "Your volume is my constant handbook, and many of my notes are written in the margins of my copy." I hastened to send a copy of this precious document to Jorgenson, and also one of my reply, in which I pointed out that our book would have been but a mediocre performance without my collaborator's excellent Franklin scholarship. And that was not false modesty on my part. Nevertheless, Van Doren's letter renewed for me a valued relationship and gave me deep satisfaction.

Columbia's graduate English faculty was a distinguished group in the second decade of the century; but none surpassed William Peterfield Trent in sensitive appreciation of literature, in patient and discriminating scholarship, or in the inspiration of the classroom. Tall, with sparse grey beard and twinkling blue eyes, he had a personality that always commanded respect, and often affection. I took his course in the seventeenth-century lyric poets, and he taught me a love for Herrick, Marvell, Lovelace, and the rest that I have never outgrown. He liked to read some of their lines in class; and after he had read a little poem of Herrick's, I have seen him take off his reading glasses and wipe them, saying, "The tears do not come to my eyes, gentlemen, because those lines are sad, but because they are beautiful." Beauty is many things of course; but the beauty of a small lyric, felt deeply, is something very precious.

Professor Trent became my adviser in my work on a dissertation. I had many long talks with him, not all of them about my studies. One day he told me: "You can waste a great deal of time cooling your heels waiting for me in office hours. Now, I have to give a lecture once a week at Hunter College, and after the lecture I am expected to spend an hour in one of the parlors over there so the girls can come in and consult with me. But they don't come in, and there I am, stranded. Why don't you come over there in my parlor hours? Then we can talk at length." It was a great opportunity. Of course I came, every week, and we did talk, at length, of many things. Trent had been a great friend of Theodore Roosevelt's and had often been one of a group at Oyster Bay on evenings or week ends. He was there once when T. R. had just received a letter from Taft, then governor of the Philippines. He read the letter aloud, with frequent exclamations of pleasure—"He's right!" "Bully for him!"—and after he had finished it, he declared soberly, "I'm going to make that man President of the United States!"

It is difficult to refrain from telling other stories of Professor Trent, for whose memory I still have so much love and respect; but I am dogged by the thought of what "Brander" said about his "anecdotage."

Here, then, is my gallery of great professors. I sat under many dull ones, too, and listened to their prosy lectures; but I prefer to leave them in the oblivion that has covered them long since. I have been fortunate in knowing so many who were worthy of their high calling, and these little "profiles" are a votive offering to the names of those great ones from a student who once sat in their classrooms.

7

Frontier Adventure

THE AIR WAS RED. The wind blew constantly, and it picked up the red dust from our streets and fields so that there was a slight haze wherever we walked. We breathed this red air, it colored our faces and hands and clothes, and it sifted into our houses and shops to lay a thin red veil on everything we touched.

But we did not mind it much. We were building an empire or something. We had the sense of being a part of great beginnings. Oklahoma and Indian Territories had just been admitted as a single state; and we were down here in the Washita Valley, upon whose fine red soil we were going to found a new farming and ranching economy that would be richer and more prosperous than anything ever before known in the Southwest. Life might be a little rough and primitive just now, but give us a few years and our valley would be filled with substantial farmers and our jerry-built towns would be splendid cities.

Such an ambitious town was Alex. The place was too small to bear the full weight and grandeur of the name Alexander; that might come later, but for the present it was satisfied to be called Alex. Small though it was, all agreed that it ought to have a newspaper to promote and advertise its advantages at home and abroad.

So a handful of advertising contracts, signed by the town's merchants, were offered, with a rent-free office building, to my elder brother if he would install a small printing plant in Alex and publish a weekly paper. Thus was born, in 1907, the *Alex Tribune*.

But before a year had passed, my brother became seriously ill; and when he was hospitalized, I was sent down to Alex by the family to dispose of the paper and to conduct it until the sale and transfer were made. I was less than a year out of the university and had recently undertaken, with my father, the publication of a weekly at Marengo, Iowa; and now I found myself suddenly in an environment as unfamiliar as it was challenging and exciting.

Alex was a town of only a few hundred, with plank sidewalks where there were any at all, with ten or a dozen stores, a bank, a pool-hall, a blacksmith shop, and the printing office. And the red wind. In the late fall it rained, and then we wore rubber boots and slithered about ankle-deep in mud.

The *Tribune* was only a four-page paper, and I did all the work on it myself—writing the news, soliciting the advertising, attending to collections, setting the type, making up the forms, getting out some job printing. All the work, that is, except turning the crank of the Campbell press on Thursdays; for that job I got a stout, good-natured colored boy for a dollar. My brother had provided some pretty good type, with which I enjoyed working. Also I had some fun writing a bit of humorous local verse occasionally, to stick into a corner of the front page with a border around it. One such, I recall, was about a jackass whose braying woke us early every morning; I thought my *jeu d'esprit* would infuriate the animal's owner and that he would at least stop his paper, but instead he was so carried away by having his jack immortalized in *Tribune* verse that he came in and bought ten extra copies.

On Saturdays our main street filled with ranchers and their families who had come in spring-wagons, cowboys in boots and spurs who had come horseback, overalled young Indians who had ridden in on their ponies, and Indian families in wagons. Alex was lively of a Saturday, what with trading, talking, show-off riding, and an occasional fight. There were no open saloons, however, and nobody wore guns.

I saw no gunplay in the classic pattern of the frontier towns of the Old West made familiar to us now on the screen. But I did see some of the most brutal fights imaginable, including kicking, gouging, biting, and some chewing on ears and noses. Here were encounters such as might have taken place, one could imagine, between animals, or representatives of one of the Pliocene anthropoid types, but scarcely between specimens of Homo sapiens. It was interesting but repulsive.

Our local badman was the blacksmith, and he made trouble only when he was drunk, which was often. He not only ran the blacksmith shop but he drove the town's dray-wagon behind a big pair of Clydesdales. When he had a few drinks under his belt, he would drive that team thundering down main street, shouting and swinging his whip in a frenzy like that of Messala trying to beat Ben Hur in a chariot race. People would leave the street clear for him, saying to each other, "Old Jock's drunk again." Sometimes Jock came into my office when he was half-seas over. He was a big fellow and he scared me silly, but I always managed to get rid of him without serious trouble. As I maneuvered him out of the office, I would keep a firm grip upon the metal "side-stick" that the printer uses in making up forms, though I could scarcely imagine ever using such a lethal weapon.

I saw another side of Jock's character one sultry afternoon in late summer. I had been told that this was cyclone weather, and a friend who lived only a few steps from my printing office had invited me to take refuge in his storm-cave if ever a twister blew up. Sure enough, on this afternoon the whirling, inverted cone of cloud appeared plainly off to the south, and I joined a lot of other people who were tumbling into my friend's cave. It was dark in there, with much confusion and the crying of children; but above it all rose a voice lifted in prayer. "Lord, save us! Lord, we believe! Lord, we believe in thee! Save us! We'll live to serve thee!" I have no idea how long we were in that cave; but after a while someone ventured to lift the door a little and found that it was raining and that the cyclone had missed Alex entirely. We all piled out of the cellar, breathing the fresh air and scarcely knowing whether to laugh or cry.

"Who was it praying in there?" I asked my friend.

"Oh, that was old Jock," he replied. "He sure gets pious when he's scared, don't he?"

I think Jock stayed sober for a month after that.

North and east of Alex was a region occupied by Indian families living on individual allotments. These families were wealthy in lands, but the Dawes Commission had broken up their way of life and ruined them. They were disoriented, aimless, and without ambition. There was no fraternization whatever between them and the whites. They came to town to trade, and our local doctor sometimes served them; but there were no interrelations in school, church, or social friendships.

The Alex doctor was always coaxing me to ride out with him on his trips through the Indian lands. He wanted company and someone to listen to his interminable tales of his life as a Don Juan of medicine. Doc was a paunchy, grey-haired fellow, as seedy and dissolute a camp-follower of Hippocrates as I ever knew. To hear him tell it, his methods with female patients were anything but orthodox. I hope he was eventually run out of town. I finally went with him on one of his trips among the Indians, to find them living in crowded and unsanitary houses, uncommunicative, apparently terrorized by sickness. As for Doc, he discoursed loudly to me on the details of each case and his diagnosis and prognosis as though we were in the lecture hall of a clinic, displaying to my reluctant gaze the diseased parts; then he dispensed some medicines, gave some directions, and collected his fee. One of those trips with Doc was enough for me.

As for social life in Alex, it seems to me there was very little of it. I played poker about once a week with the pleasant and personable sons of the proprietor of the general store, whose name was Smith; and occasionally one of the Smith boys and I would play whist with the schoolteacher and the waitress at the pool-hall lunch counter. It was the only period in my life in which I spent any considerable time at cards.

At last I found a purchaser for the *Tribune*—or rather a trader who was willing to exchange a piece of land in an adjoining county for plant, business, and goodwill. He was a handsome, well-dressed fellow, who wore a black mustache. He gave me a deed, promised to send an abstract of title immediately, got my name on a bill of sale, and was off in a cloud of red dust. I soon found that the description of the parcel of land in the deed was fictitious. And this for a boy who had studied contract law at the University of Chicago! It took me a week of lying in wait in Paul's Valley, the county seat in which the sharper lived, to catch up with him. He was continually in and out of town, and in the meantime I lived at the most primitive and wretched of country hotels. Finally I took to meeting the trains and calling at offices on a regular schedule, and one afternoon I caught up with him. He surprised me by turning over the bill of sale with a minimum of threats and cajolery on my part.

"I don't know what I'd do with it anyway," he said.

I went back to Alex and ten days later sold the *Tribune* to another purchaser, who had no black mustache but who did have some cash in hand.

All in all, I was an Alex resident for only three or four months. My experience there seems to form an episode out of context with the rest of my life. But I think it was good for me to be separated for a time from my books, family, and familiar pattern of living. It was one way of growing up.

8

The *Midland*

In the second decade of the twentieth century there was an outburst of small and individualistic periodicals that came to be known as "little magazines." Just what was this little magazine? It is difficult to "cabin, crib, confine, or bind" the lot of them within one definition. Their essence was diversity. Usually, but not always, their issues were physically "little"; very often they were short-lived, but not always; most of them, but not all, represented the voices of individual editors or of small groups. Often they gave special care to their typography and were pleasing to the eye. Nearly all of them boasted of being "noncommercial," which meant that although they charged a modest subscription price and printed advertisements when they could get them, they paid nothing to their contributors and were happy if they took in enough to pay their printers more or less regularly. Some of these little magazines were wholly devoted to poetry, some to literary criticism, some to experimental writing, some to the propagation of radical social and political doctrine. And a flock of them simply defied classification.

We still have little magazines today, of course; but they are now generally endowed by institutions or groups, and thus they differ from the highly individualized rabble of little publications, mostly rebels of one kind or another and mostly teetering on the edge of extinction, that I observed with so much interest forty and fifty years ago.

In 1915, for example, there were twelve little magazines founded, of which seven lasted for a year or less. Only two outlasted four years. Longest-lived of the twelve started in that year of 1915 was *The Midland*, of Iowa City. It is of this magazine and its editor, John Towner Frederick, that I wish to write here.

I cannot prove it, but I have long thought it probable that Josiah Royce, the Harvard philosopher, planted the seed that later flowered in the *Midland*. He came out to the State University of Iowa in 1902 to give the Phi Beta Kappa address, and on that occasion he said some things about "The Higher Provincialism" that not only attracted wide attention but made a deep impression on his audience in Iowa City. What he wanted was a genuine provincial spirit to hold the line against the encroachments of national industrialism. His utterance was an early warning against the abuses of what was later to be called "mass culture." Among his hearers, undoubtedly, was Clarke F. Ansley, head of the University's department of English, who became an exponent, year after year, of the new regionalism in American literature.

Eventually a group of Ansley's young men became imbued with the idea of founding, right there in Iowa City, a magazine of belles-lettres that might become a rallying point for midwestern culture. I must not force my thesis too far, but I seem to hear some echo of Royce in the *Midland's* first editorial: "Possibly the region between the mountains would gain in variety at least if it retained more of its makers of literature, music, pictures, and other expressions of civilization, and possibly civilization itself might be with us a somewhat swifter process if expression of its spirit were more frequent."

If the *Midland* created a sensation in the Iowa corn-lands, it was a mild one indeed. The *cognoscenti* approved, and enough sent in their names, accompanied by a dollar and a half, to encourage the young entrepreneurs. And there were encouraging words, with checks, from Chicago, from the Iowa colony in California, and even from New York. Not many checks, but enough to pay modest printing bills—or almost enough.

I read the magazine from its first number. Already an enthusiastic follower of the new midwestern literary movement, I was deeply sympathetic with what the Iowa City group was doing. The *Midland* was two years old when I wrote an article about it for my weekly newspaper, thereby attracting the attention of editor Frederick. Thus fortuitously began one of the most valued friendships of my life. Our correspondence for a few years was desultory, but in 1920, I sent him the manuscript of a short story called "The Man With the Good Face," and that eventually brought us closer together.

Most young newspaper men in those days were experimenting with novels and short stories. Many were turning out imitations of O. Henry, and I had my turn at that game. Only three of my stories had been published, however, and I had a big collection of rejection slips when I wrote the "Good Face" story. This, I felt, was something different. I sent it to a New York literary agent named Holly, with a two-dollar reading fee; and he replied, "I regret to report that I cannot see a sale for it. . . . It has an unhealthy and morbid theme." But John Frederick did not agree. He immediately accepted the story for the *Midland,* made a few helpful suggestions for improvements (he was always doing that for his contributors), and published it in his magazine in December, 1920. Then Edward J. O'Brien reprinted it in his *Best*

Short Stories volume for 1921, and anthologists picked it up from there, and so on.

But the point is that "The Man With the Good Face" got me into the *Midland* group; and when I joined the English faculty at Iowa in 1921, Frederick invited me to become an associate editor and three years later co-editor of the magazine. A little later I undertook half of the financial and management responsibility as well, though there was no transfer of ownership; the *Midland* was Frederick's. Never was there a happier partnership. The editors agreed basically in theory and nearly always in taste, and differed enough to make them checks on one another.

Fairly tall and spare in figure, with a prominent nose in a lean and irregularly fashioned face, John Frederick was no Adonis; but there was something about him that always commanded respect. I think it was Virginia Woolf who once visited the Iowa campus and later wrote in the *Freeman* or *New Republic* a piece about Frederick that described him as "Lincolnian." That rather embarrassed him, and it was not quite right because it placed him in a heroic pose unnatural to him. Nobody on the campus was less pretentious. Kindly and sympathetic, with a ready sense of humor, Frederick maintained always a certain modest reserve of dignity. Many of his students had an admiration for him that stopped just this side of idolatry.

John and I shared the task of "first reader" equally. The clearly impossible manuscripts we returned directly with rejection form 1, 2, or 3. To the others we attached notes and then exchanged them, so that both of us read those that seemed to have possibilities. Most of our reading of manuscripts was done at home, of course, and once a week we would have a consultation and make some decisions. John wrote hundreds of letters and notes to would-be contributors, scribbling them by hand; he was always understanding, sympathetic, and constructive in his suggestions. He could remove the sting from a rejection by a kind of epistolary surgery and make a young writer thank him for sending a manuscript back. I came to join in this task of correspondence with writers and found it an experience full of curious twists and surprises.

As I recall, we commonly received ten or a dozen contributions a day. Eventually, the University supplied us with a half-time assistant to do the clerical work—and sometimes more than the merely clerical. Some of these were young people of unusual talent and ability; I remember especially Harry Hartwick, Ruth Lechlitner, and Charles Brown Nelson.

One factor that helped us to attract good writers in spite of the fact that we paid nothing in cash for contributions was the consistent support of Edward J. O'Brien, who began the compilation of his yearbook of *Best Short Stories* in the year in which the *Midland* was founded. In the introduction to his first volume, O'Brien wrote:

One new periodical . . . claims unique attention this year for recent achievement and abundant future promise. A year ago a slender little monthly magazine entitled *The Midland* was first issued. It attracted very little attention, and in the course of a year published but ten short stories. It has been my pleasure and wonder to find in these ten stories the most vital interpretation in fiction of our national life that many years have been able to show. Since the most brilliant days of the New England men of letters, no such hope has proclaimed itself with such assurance and modesty.

In succeeding volumes O'Brien continued to deal kindly with the *Midland*. His yearbook was a combination anthology, index, and rating-table. He apparently read and rated thousands of stories each year. To the "distinctive" ones he awarded a star, while even better ones got two stars, and those he thought were the very best received three stars. It was a great period for the short story, and O'Brien was its prophet. To be starred in his annual was success, and to be three-starred or reprinted there was fame. Many *Midland* stories were three-starred by O'Brien, and he sometimes reprinted as many as three of them in one of his volumes. And so it came about that writers who could get cash for their stories from other magazines often sent us their manuscripts in the hope of an O'Brien accolade. Too often, it must be added, these were formula stories that did not suit us— and, by the same token, would not have pleased the discriminating O'Brien.

The *Midland* found some good authors, however; and as I glance over the twenty bound volumes on my shelves, I find myself tingling with the memory of the discoveries of those years. And I note that the magazine was never quite as regional as it had set out to be. It printed the Iowa stories of Ruth Suckow, the Missouri sketches of Raymond Weeks, the Hoosier tales of Leo L. Ward, Chicago pieces by James T. Farrell, and the Nebraska poems of Edwin Ford Piper; but also some wonderful things William March sent from New York and Leonard Cline from Baltimore and other points, poems by Haniel Long from Pittsburgh, the prose and verse of Howard Mumford Jones coming from Texas, Roland English Hartley's stories mailed from San Francisco, and poems and stories of Raymond Knister and Leyland Huckfield from Canada. Moreover, these authors moved about in this great country: Miss Suckow went to live in the East, Weeks became head of Romance Languages at Columbia and Jones dean of the graduate school at Michigan and then at Harvard,

Piper and Knister came to Iowa, and Haniel Long took up residence at Santa Fe. It was as though they were conspiring to spoof the idea of a definitely regional magazine. Meantime, the *Midland* was always delighted to print distinguished stories and good verse wherever they came from; yet it remained true to its name through its emphasis on the life of the Middle West.

I shared the editing and management of the *Midland* with John Frederick for five years. Our circulation most of the time was only about five hundred, at three dollars a year. The design and careful printing of the magazine were chiefly due to John Springer, an artist with types who had once edited a newspaper and represented his county in the state legislature. When I knew him he worked for Willis Mercer, our printer, and shambled about looking like a faded replica of Mark Twain. But he had a keen eye for the beauty of a printed page. Mercer was the most generous of printers and took a deep personal interest in the magazine; we paid him what now seems the unbelievably small sum of a hundred dollars a month, which certainly allowed him little or no profit. Thus we managed to break about even in these years. As for our own financial reward, John and I would take out twenty-five dollars apiece three or four times a year—or something like that.

But in the optimistic climate of the late twenties, it seemed to many that the *Midland* should be making more of its opportunities. In the introduction to his short story yearbook for 1930, O'Brien urged the several regional periodicals to merge with the *Midland* "to issue a full-grown national monthly of belles-lettres." He added:

If the *Midland* chooses to take the lead in this matter, I am convinced, after many years' reflection, that it has the same opportunity to crystalize the best expression of contemporary

national life that the *Atlantic Monthly* was able to seize upon
its foundation, and that *Harper's Magazine* enjoyed a generation ago. Two generations ago, Boston was the geographical
center of American literary life; one generation ago, New
York could claim pride of place; and I trust the idea will not
seem too unfamiliar if I suggest that the geographical center
today is Iowa City.

Frederick had been thinking along the same lines for a
year or more. He was not much interested in mergers,
however; and he decided, after correspondence with gen-
erous-sounding friends in Chicago, to move the *Midland*
to that metropolis. Here was the great city of the Midwest, which had recently developed strong enough groups
to support the art museum, the symphony orchestra, the
magazine *Poetry*, and other cultural institutions.

I was by this time deeply engaged with the School
of Journalism at Iowa and could not think of accompany-
ing the magazine in its great adventure. I could only give
it my blessing and the promise to stay on as an associate
editor. John and I dissolved our partnership as informally as we had initiated it, without payments, promises, or
documents.

In Chicago the *Midland* was for a time livelier and
more attractive than ever before. Esther Paulus Frederick became co-editor. But the crash of falling stocks,
the closing of banks, and the abrupt end of an era of
buoyancy and sanguine expectations had combined to
greet the magazine on its coming to the big town.
Chicago friends who had spoken generous words in greeting it suddenly added up their assets and found words
were all they had to be generous with. "The fourth year
of the depression proves to be one year too many for the
Midland," wrote Frederick in June, 1933, as he sent off
the copy for the last issue.

Henry L. Mencken once made the statement that the *Midland* was "probably the most important literary magazine ever established in America." This was typical Menckenese, of course; but there was a time when the magazine—"our" magazine, I like to call it—stood very high in the estimation of many discriminating critics. I was fully rewarded for the many hours of work I gave it by the satisfaction of helping to publish some good literature and making friendships that I still value.

I realize that all I have here written of John Frederick has been in the past tense and that this may have given the impression that he has shuffled off by now this mortal coil. By no means. I have been telling of a departed time, not a departed man. Frederick has written two distinguished novels of midwestern life—*Druida* and *Green Bush*—and he has followed his bent for farming on a big place in Alcona County, Michigan. For a time he was associated with the "Contemporary Thought" program at Northwestern University, also acting occasionally as a visiting lecturer at Notre Dame. Later he made a custom of serving half a year at the latter university and spending the other half on the farm; then, after the death of Father Ward, he was named head of the very lively English department there. After his retirement, now imminent, he will doubtless continue and expand his writing, which has been, for John Frederick, a lifelong and compulsive activity.

9

The Society for the Prevention of Cruelty to Speakers

THERE IS ENTIRELY TOO MUCH speech-making in the world today. Bad and mediocre speech-making I mean, of course; and that includes most of it. Every service club the country over must, for some occult reason, have a half-hour speech after each weekly luncheon. Every church group must call for a sermon at least once a week, not because its minister has anything new to say or any talent for saying it, but because custom forces him to be a preacher as well as a pastor. College classes listen to interminable lectures when the matter discussed could be presented far better in print, on the screen, or through laboratory demonstration. Political leaders and would-be leaders pour forth endless streams of double talk. Professional lecturers ply their tricks. Persons who have achieved notoriety for this or that take to the platform. And incidentally, what is so useless, what is so vain, nugatory, tiresome, and unprofitable as a commencement address? But we must have them: we must have all of this speech-making, and more. One famous "system" blankets the United States with its classes to teach every man to be an "effective" speaker, for such a stupendous flow of talk requires constant recruitment of talkers. Thus nearly everybody becomes a public speaker at some time or other, whether or not he really has anything to say.

I think I must some day make a speech about it all.

Certainly I have made my own contribution—and no small one—to this universal abuse. I remember well sitting on the platform of a church where a high-school commencement was being held and hearing a local minister addressing God through an "invocation" in the familiar fashion affected by some preachers: "O Lord, we have had a busy day, first with the exhibitions in the school rooms, then with the junior exercises, and then at the picnic in the schoolhouse yard, and now here at the commencement program. And we pray that as soon as the speaker here has finished, we may go to our homes in peace and quiet to refreshing sleep. Amen." The words were addressed to the Lord; but the hint was intended for the speaker, and I did my best to follow it. I think the best speech I ever made was one to a Rotary Club that had asked me to discuss "Freedom of the Press" during Newspaper Week. I shall favor my readers with the entire speech herewith: "Mr. President, Gentlemen of the Rotary Club: There is no such thing as freedom of the press. I thank you." Then I sat down, to the consternation of the program chairman. Of course I spoiled it all later by yielding to the urging of the president to go on and say something about it anyway, and I talked for a while about the nature of freedom and the controls to which the press is subject. It would have served me right and paid me well for my smart-aleck "hamming" if the Rotarians had all walked out immediately after I had sat down, but they were so intrigued by the spectacle of a man who actually appeared not to want to make a speech that they stayed it out.

Now, I am convinced that the blame for this vast sea of mediocre speechifying should not be laid upon the speech-makers, but upon the audiences who demand it. It has become conventional to require speeches on all occasions, whether or not anything really needs to be said at length. Moreover, it is an American tradition that whenever a man achieves some fame or some degree of note, he must be dragged to the platform whether he is a good or bad performer thereon. The chain by which he is thus dragged is made of dollars and is therefore hard to break. And so Ralph Waldo Emerson, who admitted that he was born with a pen rather than a tongue, long earned much of his living by lecturing; Horace Greeley, who cut a poor figure on the platform and repelled hearers by his squeaky voice, and who once confessed to Henry Ward Beecher that he always considered a lecture successful if half his audience stayed through to the end, was a platform "star" for many years. Even good speakers, moreover, have often loathed the platform because of the strains of travel, the discomforts of bad hotels and irregular meals, and the treatment of inconsiderate hosts and lecture committees.

I personally have little commiseration to spare for bored and restless audiences; they have brought their punishment upon themselves. Save your pity, say I, for the poor speaker, harried from platform to platform, ineptly introduced, suffering from indigestion and hoarseness and supertensions.

All this is by way of general introduction to the history of the Society for the Prevention of Cruelty to Speakers. For specific introduction, I must go back to the latter years of the *Midland* magazine at Iowa City and the group of writers in the faculty and student body of the State University of Iowa at the end of the 1920's.

John Frederick and I, who edited that magazine, agreed that we would all profit by a kind of friendly communion with some of the leading American writers of our time if we could get them to come out to Iowa City, not as orators or lecturers but as our guests for conversations, some counsel and advice, and a little after-luncheon talk. The luncheon audience would be small and the atmosphere informal. I think we called the sponsoring organization the Saturday Luncheon Club, which sounded harmless enough.

It is remarkable how easy it was to get the men we most wanted, and for small fees. Frederick was a persuasive fellow, and many of our notables were interested in the *Midland.* We were never able to get Henry Mencken; but we did get Sherwood Anderson and Joseph Wood Krutch and e.e. cummings and John V. A. Weaver and Leonard Cline and Robert Frost and Carl Sandburg and others. Perhaps one or two of those I name were guests of a later incarnation of our club, because when Frederick took the *Midland* to Chicago at the end of 1930 I continued the procession with a Journalism Dinner Club for a season or two before founding our famous Times Club. But more of these anon.

We spent unforgettable hours with these visitors of ours. Fixed in my memory is a picture of Frost sitting on the small of his back in an easy chair after his talk and his readings, holding a glass of milk in his hand, and regaling us between sips with amusing Amherst legends about such diverse characters as Emily Dickinson and Calvin Coolidge—wonderful stories! And Sandburg intoning folk songs to the accompaniment of his guitar. And Anderson gathered with students before a fireplace, chatting. His talk, too, was mild and easy, though his ideas were sometimes explosive.

An early speaker to one of our clubs sponsored by the School of Journalism was the novelist O. E. Rölvaag. Another early comer was Henry A. Wallace, not at that time famous in politics. He brought with him an editor of *Wallace's Farmer*, Donald R. Murphy. "Seems like Donald and I never have time to settle the problems of the world at home," said Henry, "so I thought we'd do it on the road down from Des Moines." They therefore drove down in a decrepit Model "T" Ford at a speed of twenty-five to thirty miles an hour, but they got an early start and arrived on time.

The Times Club was organized in 1934. Harry Hartwick, who liked naming things, was godfather to it. Its membership was limited to three hundred, to insure small audiences. Each member paid two dollars and was given a ticket admitting him to whatever meetings the club had for that year. We did not promise any specific program: we told them we thought we could get five or six interesting persons to visit us—not orators or professional platform men, but persons who had done things, and had ideas, and were willing to talk informally to a small audience of intelligent and sympathetic listeners. Watch the papers, we said, and you will see who they are and when they are to be here; that will be your sole notification of the meetings. At this distance, I find it hard to understand how we hypnotized three hundred Iowa Citians in those "depression" years to invest two dollars apiece in a hypothetical course of this character, but the ticket sale always went over easily.

I carried on a wide correspondence with many prospects, utilizing all of my own contacts and those of my friends to interest the kind of persons we wanted to visit us. Since we were not far from Chicago, many of our eastern friends made a visit to that metropolis include a side-trip to Iowa City. Eventually many came without asking any fee whatever, though we commonly paid a fifty-dollar honorarium and in a few cases stretched it to a hundred or even a hundred and fifty. But mostly our visitors came because they were interested in us.

One Sunday evening Lincoln Steffens called me from the hotel. "Well, I'm here," he said. "Come on down and let's have some talk." I had met him a couple of years before, when we were both on the program of a women's club federation convention; but his wife, Ella Winter, was the featured speaker, and while she was "doing her stuff," Steffens and I had a long talk about many things in the hotel lobby. At that time I invited Steffens to stop off and visit us at Iowa City on one of his frequent trips between his home at Carmel, California, and New York, and he said he would. I had renewed my invitation now and then by correspondence; and now here he was, as he said, asking me to come down to the hotel and continue our conversation where we had left off some two years earlier. But I got a group of students together and we had a late supper with him, and he discussed social and political questions with us until after midnight. His Times Club talk the following evening was a typical success for that group. Steffens was a small man with an inadequate voice; he was by no means a master of the platform, but he had a steady flow of ideas, and before a small audience in an informal atmosphere he was immensely stimulating.

We had Frost again, and Sandburg again, but it was Christopher Morley's visit in the spring of 1934 that really opened our eyes to the needs and possibilities of the Times Club operation. That and Grant Wood's ever-active genius for original projects. Grant was now coming down from his studio-home in Cedar Rapids twice a week to lecture at the University, and I was having lunch with him every Tuesday at "Smitty's" Cafe. He had become interested in the Times Club and had helped me to get Morley as a visitor. A few weeks earlier Grant had been in New York and Morley had given a cocktail party for him; now Wood wanted to return the courtesy with a party in a typical Iowa setting—but what was available? Not a lounge at the University Union, not "Smitty's," not a private house; these lacked the proper atmosphere. Finally we fixed upon a log-cabin road-house across the river. We had a good time, but the place was not right; we wanted something with distinctive connotations of our own brand of hospitality—something symbolic of the special kind of junto the Times Club was and the performance it stood for. We had felt this lack in our entertainment of other guests, but the visit of Christopher Morley seemed to point up our shortcomings and stir us to action.

We enlarged the executive committee of the club to sixteen members, and this group I dubbed "The Society for the Prevention of Cruelty to Speakers." Immediately the S.P.C.S. set out to do three things: find a home for itself, furnish such a place suitably, and devise a type of program that would entertain and amuse the guests of the Times Club and be fun for us all.

We considered various places that we might buy or rent as a home. We looked over an abandoned country schoolhouse near town, a big haymow in a well-built barn, an ancient flour-mill; and we enjoyed planning remodeling jobs. But nearly everything we considered involved financing that was too ambitious for us. Then Roland Smith—the "Smitty" of our favorite eating rendezvous and the friend of all of us—came forward with the solution. One of his speculations in Texas oil wells had recently come through with a gusher, and he was feeling even more generous than usual. He offered us, rent free, with all facilities furnished, and for as long as we wanted it, the full floor above his cafe. We could have carte blanche to do with it whatever we chose. And so the S.P.C.S. had a home, accessible, unencumbered with debt, ready for our devices.

What we resolved to do was to furnish this space as two rooms—a dining room and a parlor—all in what Grant affectionately called "the worst style of the late Victorian period." We put an ingrain carpet on the floor and a flowered paper on the walls. We decorated with Currier and Ives prints; a fine chromo of that old favorite, "Rock of Ages," in which a lady clings to the foot of a cross on a great rock lashed by foam-tipped waves from the sea; embroidered mottoes, "God Bless Our Home," "Peace Be With You," and so on; and certain designs under glass formed from the hair of some dear departed. In the dining-room section a big table was covered with a red-and-white checkered cloth, and a bulging sideboard stood in one corner. In the parlor was much red plush and walnut furniture—Boston rockers, and love seats on either side of the marble fireplace. One big chair was made of steers' horns, with seat, back, and tassels of green plush. A cottage organ, with elaborately carved walnut case and music rack, proved highly useful at our parties. Upon a marble-topped stand stood a red-plush album, which, in the course of time, came to be filled with specially posed pictures of our guests and our members.

That picture-taking stunt was fun. We bought some false beards and mustaches from a costume house and picked up some old-fashioned hats, collars, ties, and coats; and with these we would dress up our visitors and photograph them for our red-plush album. Thus we got Grant Wood with mustache and sweeping sideburns posed with his bearded friend Thomas Hart Benton in a highly artificial photograph-gallery posture beneath a framed motto, "Home, Sweet Home." We got Stephen Vincent Benét in choker collar, ascot tie, and sideburns. We got John Erskine, then at the height of his fame as Columbia lecturer on epic poetry and author of the best seller *Helen of Troy,* in an extraordinary flowing white beard; Sigmund Spaeth at the organ with a soulful expression and a bartender's mustache; Mackinlay Kantor with a black beard as wildly luxuriant as that of any cartoonist's version of a Russian nihilist; John Towner Frederick as a bearded farmer in work-jacket and broad-brimmed hat, with pitchfork in hand; Gilbert Seldes drinking tea from a mustache-cup in order to protect the fine hirsute decorations on his upper lip. And so on and so on. We hesitated to suggest to Nicholas Roosevelt, a dignified statesman of a man, that he submit himself to this childish game; but as soon as he saw what the red-plush album already contained, he exclaimed, "Oh, aren't you going to take a picture of me for that gallery?" So we got him in a "kady" hat, beard, stiff collar, and all.

The chief function of the S.P.C.S. was, of course, to give after-lecture parties to our visitors. Each member of the group was allowed to bring two guests, and our rooms were always filled. There were sandwiches from downstairs on the table, ice buckets with bottles of soft drinks and beer, and pots of coffee; we never served "hard liquor." Almost always, conversation began with our guests' exclamations about the furnishings of our rooms. "Oh, my aunt had a decoration piece of peacock feathers just like that in her front parlor! And it was set on just such a marble-topped stand!" We came to expect and to await with pleasure such an uprush of nostalgic memories on the part of every middle-aged visitor who saw our little exhibition for the first time.

Nearly always there was an informal program of some kind or other. Sometimes the company merely gathered about our guest, sitting on chairs or on the floor, and drew him out with questions. Usually there was some singing of the old songs of the nineties, with Dorothy Pownall, newspaperwoman and one of our members, at the organ. When Spaeth was with us, he sat at the organ all evening, leading the choruses and singing solos himself from a wonderful repertoire of sentimental songs of the nineties. "Steamboat Bill" Peterson, later superintendent of the Iowa Historical Society, used to lead us in one of those old repetitive songs in comic German dialect:

> *Bill:* Ist das nicht der Gartenhaus?
> *Chorus: Ja, das ist der Gartenhaus!*
> *Bill:* Und es hat ein roof on top!
> *Chorus: Ja, es hat ein roof on top!*
> *All* (fortissimo): Roof on top; Gartenhaus!
> Oh, wie schönus! Oh, magnolius!
> Oh, wie schönus Gartenhaus!

and so on and on, with prompt-pictures as guides to the chorus.

Sometimes someone would take the floor with a recitation. I shall never forget the fervor with which Mackinlay Kantor recited "The Rebel's Prayer" at a party we gave him. Occasionally (semi-occasionally, perhaps) I read "The Face on the Bar Room Floor" with melodramatic passion, turning my back on the audience after the introductory part for a quick costume and facial change before assuming the bum's character as he tells his sad story. And sometimes the two Helens (Reich

and Dawson) and Vera Mott and Bessie Hart would re-
tell in swaying unison the pathetic tale beginning:

> 'Twas a cold and stormy evening
> When our Nellie went away . . . .

Our S.P.C.S. membership, which was always kept at
or near sixteen, was divided among faculty, students, and
townspeople.   I think our first president was Evans
Worthley, Unitarian minister, though a little later we
made it a rule always to elect a student to that position.
Tom Yoselof, now a New York book publisher, was our
first student president, as I recall.   The young city
editors of the community's two daily newspapers were
active members, and the Times Club and S.P.C.S. owed
much of their success to the "play" our activities always
received in the papers.   Frederick Kent, best of university
photographers, was a faithful member, always on hand
with camera ready to take pictures for the album.

But the three wheel-horses of the organization were
Grant Wood, artist; Clyde Hart, sociologist; and Frank
Mott, eager beaver.   We owed much to the original ideas
and the contributions in time and energy of Wood and
to the lively initiative and industry of Hart.   I kept track
of the finances, the Times Club schedules, and this and
that.   I still carried on a furious correspondence with
possible guests.   We prepared a beautifully printed
"flier" which was in effect a whimsical invitation to come
and visit us, address the Times Club, and see if the
Society for the Prevention of Cruelty to Speakers lived
up to its name.   This carried a charming decoration in
the style of the nineties showing a hand pouring water
from a rose-decorated pitcher into a hobnail-glass
tumbler.   Grant Wood made the original as a pen-and-ink
drawing, and we reproduced it on the cover of our

brochure. But more effective than anything else in bringing desirable visitors our way was the talk that got about among writers and artists about our activities; the *Saturday Review of Literature* and the *New York Herald-Tribune* printed pieces about us, and soon the S.P.C.S. was being mentioned here and there in other newspapers and magazines and even in books.

I have named a number of our famous guests, but I am not going to attempt a complete list of them here. I ought not to omit mention of several Negroes whom it was our pleasure to hear and to entertain. I think the first of these was W. C. Handy, composer of the "St. Louis Blues" and other great popular pieces. He was accompanied by Rosamund Johnson, himself a musician of importance, who was a great help to the almost blind Handy in his appearance before our club. A group of students had improvised a small orchestra, which was seated on the stage, and the boys were thrilled to have the great Handy conduct them in a somewhat ragged rendition of his famous "Blues." Rosamund's brother, James Weldon Johnson, then known as the "dean" of Negro poets, was a later guest, as were the poets Countée Cullen and Langston Hughes. Hotels made some difficulty about these visitors, and we took them into our own homes. I well remember sitting up late with Cullen in my study at home reading the manuscript of what was to be his first published novel, *One Way to Heaven*.

And finally, I must say something about the guest who brought us more publicity than any of the others, but who never came. This was Gertrude Stein. When we learned that Miss Stein and her alter ego Alice B. Toklas were contemplating a visit to the United States in the fall of 1934, we at once began trying to interest her in talking to the Times Club and being the guest of the

S.P.C.S. Rousseau Voorhies, of the Macmillan Company, was most helpful in suggesting approaches. Among other things, we organized an "A Rose Is A Rose Club," had ourselves photographed at a dinner of that organization (its one and only meeting) and sent a picture of the dinner party, with all of us wearing white roses, to Miss Stein. She yielded to our blandishments and consented to come to us, for a very reasonable fee, on the evening of December 10. But by the time she had reached New York she had quarreled violently with Voorhies and wired me to know if we had any connection with him. When I reassured her on that point, she wired me again to know if we were keeping the audience small. When I told her we always kept our audiences small, she sent me another telegram to find out how small. Between us, we kept Western Union busy for a day or two; but she finally said all right, she was coming, and she would speak on "The Making of the Making of Americans." We were besieged with requests for tickets after every seat was taken. Dorothy Pownall had a story in the *Des Moines Tribune* in which she said, "Those who have thought it hard to get tickets to world series games have never encountered a real ticket shortage. They ought to try to get into the Gertrude Stein lecture." Came the tenth of December and one of those great sleet storms under which Iowa sometimes suffers. But our audience braved it all, some driving more than a hundred miles over icy roads. The audience was there, all of it, with perhaps a few more than the stipulated number; but the Misses Stein and Toklas, who had been scheduled to arrive by special plane in the early evening, were not there. About eight-thirty a Western Union boy arrived at our crowded lecture hall with the last of the series of telegrams from Miss Stein. It read: PLANE GROUNDED

WAUKESHA WISCONSIN. GERTRUDE STEIN. I allowed our Student President Yoselof the honor of breaking the news to the audience. He did it very well, and the audience took it all in good part. . . . A guest is a guest is not a guest.

The Times Club and its auxiliary, the Society for the Prevention of Cruelty to Speakers, gave us a grand hayride while they lasted. But they were too successful. The University Lecture Committee felt that its course had lost prestige through this upstart, which was always able to grab the headlines. Wheels turned within wheels, as they will in the operation of a great university, and eventually I was called into a summit conference with the president and the chairman of the Lecture Committee. I was not actually on the summit level, I am afraid, and I compromised by agreeing to a moratorium for the Times Club to last a year. My friends tell me I gave in too easily, and probably I did.

Later the club was revived briefly. The S.P.C.S. rooms were maintained for a while, then fell into disuse, and the furniture was placed in storage and much of it disappeared. A few years later, Grant Wood died, Clyde Hart joined the University of Chicago faculty, and I was called to Missouri.

But I like to think that we did something, in that place and time, toward making the lecture platform a little more justifiable and rational and that we helped to alleviate the hard lot of the public speaker. Anyway, many people, guests and hosts alike, enjoyed the experiment.

10

Education for Journalism

"OF ALL HORNED CATTLE, I want least to see in my office a college graduate!" So Horace Greeley is said to have exclaimed in a moment of exasperation. This attitude of the famous editor points us back to a time when a college education was not only something very different from what it became later but also harder to come by and intended mainly for the clergy and a few ambitious teachers and lawyers. Greeley himself had almost no formal education; he attended a country school irregularly for five or six years before he went into a printing office at eleven.

If anyone had made a survey of the educational backgrounds of the leaders of the American press at the time of Greeley's death in 1872, he would have found very few of them holding college degrees. But it may be pointed out that if our investigator had also examined the records of the men who had occupied up to that time the exalted position of President of the United States, he would have found that half of them could not display sheepskins with their names engrossed thereon.

Things changed in the 1870's. The universities changed, attitudes changed, newspapers changed. Whitelaw Reid (Miami, '56), who succeeded Greeley as editor of the *New York Tribune,* denied that his predecessor had ever made such an uncouth remark as the one about horned cattle and pointed out that by 1875 there was "scarcely a writer" on his paper who was not a college graduate. And the same was true, he thought, with his New York contemporaries, the *World,* the *Times,* and the *Evening Post.* He should have added the *Sun,* for Dana's liking for bright young men from the colleges was well known.

Many things changed in the seventies, but attitudes toward higher education were not revolutionized all at once. Many cherished the old prejudice against the "college boy." In fact, there are still some Greeleys in the newspaper offices of today—a hundred years later. But now the old-timers are likely to loose their ire not so much upon college graduates generally as upon graduates of schools of journalism. They seem to think that specialized education for journalism, one of the younger disciplines, is a more vulnerable target in these latter days. As of course it is.

We have set Greeley up as spokesman of the no-college newspaper men; and we may name Henry Watterson, of the *Louisville Courier-Journal,* as a leading exponent of the early opposition to formal education for journalism. "There is but one school of journalism," pontificated "Marse Henry," "and that is a well conducted newspaper office." This dictum was repeated in varying forms for a long time and is still heard occasionally.

It may be amusing and even instructive to trace the development of the idea of specialized education for journalism. Here was no steady march of principle, but a halting series of experimental attempts, a hassle of debate abounding in sarcasm and only occasionally marked by bold idealism, with not a little advance and retreat on both sides. I shall note here a few highlights from the record.

Watterson's statement was called forth by the first project definitely looking toward specialized education for journalism. In 1869 President Robert E. Lee, of Washington College, later Washington and Lee University, invited young men "intending to make practical printing and journalism their business in life" to accept scholarships for the college's regular course, paying for their tuition and fees by an hour's work each day in a printing office. This work was described as "disciplinary," and the name of the employing printer was carried for a few years in the college's catalog as a member of the faculty; but there was no credit course in journalism—or in printing, for that matter. "General Lee would have made a great failure if he had attempted to found a course for journalism in his University," declared Frederic Hudson, former managing editor of the *New York Herald*. And so most newspaper men thought.

But General Lee had made a dynamic suggestion. He had started editors all over the country talking about courses for journalists, editorial colleges, schools of journalism, and the like. Nearly all were against them, to be sure, but the idea would not die down; with growing frequency an editor here and there said, "Why not try it?" At the bottom of such agitation was a dissatisfaction with newspaper performance and personnel. Never had there been so much criticism of the press in magazines, in pulpits, and on the platform, as there was in the seventies and eighties.

Whitelaw Reid lifted his voice repeatedly in favor of professional standards for journalism, and that seemed to mean educated editors. He made a notable address on "Schools of Journalism" at the University of the City

of New York in 1872, which may have hastened steps
taken soon thereafter at Cornell University. There, under the enlightened leadership of Andrew D. White, a
Certificate in Journalism was offered for the completion
of a prescribed liberal arts curriculum plus some work
in the University's printing department. This was perhaps an advance on the Lee plan; but, like that project,
it was never fully realized. Out in Missouri a St. Louis
newspaper man, David R. McAnally, joined the faculty
of the State University and in 1879 offered a "special
study" course in the history and practice of journalism
which ran for six years. This was the first credit course
with a definite "Journalism" label to be given in any
university.

But these were generally regarded as eccentric instances by both educators and editors. Journalistic ability
was a "gift," argued the erudite Edwin Lawrence Godkin
(Belfast, '51), first in the *Nation* and later when he became editor of the *New York Evening Post:* therefore
education for journalism was absurd. A large part of the
"working press" agreed with him. After all, these editors
had themselves received no such special academic training, and see what they had done! The very suggestion
of schools of journalism seemed to be (and doubtless in
some degree was) a criticism of them and their achieve-
ments.

Nevertheless, the idea slowly gained adherents. Some
twenty years after Lee's famous gesture, Eugene M.
Camp, of the *Philadelphia Times,* wrote to some of the
leading editors of the country, asking whether they would
approve the establishment of schools of journalism. The
replies were sharply divided, but a number were favor-
able. And some were surprising! Who is this who
writes, "A school of special instruction in newspaper work

is feasible and desirable"? None other than "Marse
Henry" Watterson, of Louisville—too wise a man not to
be capable of changing his mind as the times changed.
Camp's efforts resulted in the action of the University of
Pennsylvania by which the first organized curriculum in
journalism education was set up, in the Wharton School.
Throughout most of the nineties this work was ably
directed by Joseph French Johnson, a scholar and an
experienced newspaper editor.

Another and more powerful newspaperman who did
not agree that journalists were born rather than made
was Joseph Pulitzer, of the *New York World*. Early in
the nineties he proposed to Columbia University the
establishment of a school of journalism, but the reply was
not enthusiastic. He mulled the matter over in his mind
for some ten years, and then presented to Presidents
Low of Columbia and Eliot of Harvard a summary of his
conclusions. It was Low's response that won Pulitzer's
approval, with attached prize of two million dollars.
Eliot was more cautious, but education for journalism
was in line with his thinking on the practical curriculum,
and he became a member of the "board of advisers" for
the new school at Columbia, and in that capacity suggested a curriculum which included six courses: Newspaper Administration, Newspaper Manufacture, Law of
Journalism, Ethics of Journalism, History of Journalism,
and Literary Forms. When plans for the school at Columbia were announced in 1903, they evoked such a
chorus of carping criticism that Pulitzer wrote an article
for the *North American Review* defending the project and
the whole theory of education for journalism. Most of
the objections, he declared, were founded upon "prejudice
and ignorance." The school that Pulitzer established with

his munificent gift was opened in 1912, the year after the founder's death, with Talcott Williams as its first dean.

Meantime the idea had been spreading. Courses in journalism had been initiated in several midwestern state universities in the nineties—Kansas, Iowa, Indiana, Michigan, Nebraska. Soon sequences in journalism appeared: Frank W. Scott was busy at Illinois, W. G. Bleyer at Wisconsin, Merle Thorpe at Washington. Beginning in 1902, the University of Chicago conducted for ten years a sequence for journalists which included a course called "Development and Organization of the Press," taught by Dean George E. Vincent and dropped when he went to the University of Minnesota to become its president.

Here I think I must interrupt my historical narrative to wonder if a later president of the University of Chicago, Robert M. Hutchins, ever heard of this ignoble episode in his institution's history. I once heard Hutchins make an address before the Inland Press Association in which he likened schools of journalism to "barber colleges" and "schools for beauticians." Like some others, I resented this at the time as an insult both to a great profession and to a considerable body of sincere educators. But I received new light on the Hutchins attitude some years later, when I found occasion to challenge, from the floor of a convention in Philadelphia, his knowledge of what the schools were doing. I supported my charge by citing some remarks he had just made about hypothetical courses in "Advanced Proofreading"; and this brought the Chancellor to his feet protesting that I must not take his witticisms for serious comment. "Doctor Hutchins," I said, "we are often at a loss to distinguish between your wit and your wisdom." I now think that the Inland Press observation was intended as a witticism and that most of the Hutchins talk against schools of journalism was not as serious as it sometimes sounded. It was, of course, a part of his crusade against vocational training in the universities.

I have two other highlights to mention in the early development of education for journalism. In 1908 George Harvey, editor of *Harper's Weekly*, delivered the Bromley Lectures at Yale on the subject, "Journalism, Politics, and the University"; and therein he dared to assert baldly that journalism could be taught as well in college halls as in newspaper offices, and indeed better. What a pother of commentary that created in the press! But, on the whole, derision was less noticeable than might have been expected; sympathy with some kind of specialized education for journalism clearly was increasing. Yale, however, established no school of journalism, perhaps because Colonel Harvey offered no two-million-dollar gift to support his thesis.

It was in the year of Harvey's lectures at Yale that the first fully organized school of journalism, with a bachelor's degree, opened its doors. This was at the University of Missouri. The late Forrest O'Dell, in his Columbia thesis on the early history of journalism education, asserts that the Missouri school was founded on the plan of President Eliot, of Harvard; and it was indeed established along those lines. But the pioneer school had been promoted by the Missouri Press Association, and its founding fathers were Missourians. Its first dean was Walter Williams, a newspaperman of experience and an able organizer. Years later I came to know Williams in connection with the work of our professional associations and to respect him highly, as we all did.

My own first awareness of all this growth of sentiment for specialized education in journalism, which I have been tracing, came when I was conducting a weekly newspaper in Iowa and some pipe-dreamers suggested that we ought to try out the new scheme in our own state university. I was against it, and I said so unhesitatingly in my editorial column. I stood with Henry Watterson in his early conviction that a newspaper office was the place to learn newspaper work. Beyond question, my objections were founded, as Pulitzer had said most of the arguments against schools of journalism were, upon "prejudice and ignorance." And also, I have no doubt, upon a certain feeling of injured pride: "I've never attended a school of journalism, but look what I'm doing! Pretty good, isn't it?" Today I confess my error with appropriate shame and in metaphorical sackcloth and ashes.

And I hasten to say that I was not so blinded by this "prejudice and ignorance" that I could not correct my mistakes as I learned more about education for journalism. I followed at some distance the amazing development of the movement. By 1917, when I went to Columbia University and enrolled for graduate work in English, the number of colleges and universities throughout the country offering courses in journalism exceeded fifty; more than half of these institutions had such work organized into special schools or departments, while the others carried their journalism instruction forward in their departments of English. At Columbia I took only one course in the School of Journalism, but I had opportunities of observing the work there and in other places. And so, when I was invited to head the small English department at Simpson College and found there a group of students eager to learn something about newspapers, their backgrounds, and how to write for them, I decided to experiment, offer a course or two, and get the "feel" of teaching journalism.

I liked the "feel," but I still had only a shadowy

notion of what education for journalism was all about. Soon the State University at Iowa City called me to its faculty, not to teach journalism but American literature and short-story writing. There I found a very young school of journalism, directed by a professor of classical archeology who was also an administrator of genius and tireless energy. Such a man in a university community is a predestined victim of overwork; and when Doctor Charles H. Weller staggered to his death under an overload of administrative jobs, it became necessary to find three or four men to succeed him. In a curiously roundabout fashion, the president of the University learned that he had in his own English department an ambitious young man named Mott who had been brought up in a newspaper office and who might be made over into a journalism teacher and administrator. So he took me in hand and sent me on a tour of eight or ten of the more important journalism schools.

That was a great experience for me. At last I learned what the leaders in education for journalism were trying to do, and on my return from this survey I was able to formulate for the faculty of the School of Journalism at Iowa the philosophy behind the efforts of the schools I had visited. I shall return to this "philosophy" later, but I think I should note here that there was at that time a greater proportionate stress on the technical processes of the craft of journalism than there came to be later. This was the answer of the schools to the early Watterson objection (still loudly proclaimed by many critics) that such things could be taught only in the newspaper office. Some of us, under this pressure, probably overemphasized our laboratories at the expense of general arts and sciences in the twenties.

There were three great leaders in education for

journalism in those days—Walter Williams, of Missouri; John W. Cunliffe, of Columbia; and W. G. Bleyer, of Wisconsin. That triumvirate commanded our respect, ran our American Association of Schools and Departments of Journalism, and trained many of the young men who were to become the second generation of leaders in our field. Though they did not always agree among themselves, they led our thinking on the problems of our new discipline.

When I knew him, Williams was a handsome, white-haired gentleman of force and charm. When he was on the platform, his oratory had a golden quality in which his personal philosophy was an important element; at the conference table he was authoritative and cogent; among his friends, he was genial and helpful. Cunliffe was of a slender, rather tall figure, had sharp eyes that seemed to look into your mind, but was modest and friendly. He always impressed me with his thoughtfulness and wisdom. His was a background of scholarship in English literature, and he was a busy author and editor. Willard Grosvenor Bleyer was a smaller man, wore a professorial Vandyke beard, and took things seriously. He had built a fine school at Wisconsin and was training some of the best young men in the country in his graduate seminars. He was the first educator in the journalism field to attempt accreditation of schools and departments; this he did through our national association's Council on Education, which he headed for many years. That he was unsuccessful in putting his complete system into effect was a deep disappointment to him—but all that was to come later. Bleyer was a pioneer in many senses, beloved by his students, respected by his colleagues.

There were other stalwarts, of course, in the schools of journalism of the mid-twenties. James Melvin Lee, of New York University, was a gentleman and a scholar and conducted a matchless review department in *Editor & Publisher* entitled "The World of Books." Eric W. Allen, at the University of Oregon, was a great teacher as well as a good scholar. A. L. Stone, who was dean of the Montana school, was popular among us all and served for years as secretary of our national association. Harry Center, veteran journalist, was a notable figure at Boston University. I can name here only a few men of that time who stand out prominently in my memory.

My own chief activity in education for journalism covered thirty years, divided equally between the Universities of Iowa and Missouri. At Iowa in those early days (they do things better now) we were ill equipped and badly housed. But we had a good laboratory newspaper, an able though small faculty, and a really wonderful run of students. I could glorify these pages with the names of a few of them, but I shall restrain my pride in them.

Transferring to Missouri was accepting a challenge. Here I found a remarkable body of tradition, a great loyalty to the school, and generous support from the administration. The laboratory newspaper was unique; owned by the alumni, circulating more in the city than on the campus, it had to stand on its own legs like any professional newspaper.

I made the change at a time when we had to cope, in our small way, with great events. The United States had entered the Second World War a few months earlier, and the whole pattern of our operations had to change abruptly.

We got along marvelously well on the technical side. As with all newspapers in war times, supplies and renewal of equipment presented great difficulties. I found on my arrival a critical need for some new linotypes, and it was not easy to obtain the government approval then necessary for such a purpose. It was a happy day when we got our new linotypes and some new type and I had my heart's desire in seeing the *Missourian* in modern "streamlined" dress. We had to look sharply, too, even amid all the anxieties of the times, toward an imperative expansion of our instructional program into such technical fields as photojournalism, radio, facsimile, and so on.

But there were even more vital changes in our pattern. The war and its aftermath brought startling changes in our courses and requirements, in our student body, and in the atmosphere of the school. We had to shift quickly to an "accelerated curriculum" to enable boys going into the service to finish, whenever possible, before the army called them. And then suddenly we found our classes made up of more than three-fourths girls, instead of the customary less than one-fourth. This was the "paper-doll" era. Only eleven men were graduated in our class of 1944, along with forty-seven women.

But as soon as the war was over, the men came flooding in, hundreds upon hundreds of them, eager and in a hurry to make up for lost time, waving the "GI Bill of Rights" in their hands. Our two modest buildings and our struggling laboratories were crammed to their limits and past. My own lecture course in "History and Principles of Journalism" was literally homeless for a week at the beginning of the fall term of 1946. Too large to find even standing-room in our own auditorium, the class met a time or two in the basement of the Methodist Church. But, understandably enough, we were not welcome there, and I tried unsuccessfully to get into a movie theater. Eventually, we occupied the concert room of the old music building, where I lectured three times a week to

the accompaniment of pianos above us and flutes, saxo-
phones, and drums behind us. The next year, with an
enrollment of about five hundred, we met in the University auditorium. These were busy, harried months when
we were doing the best we could for twice as many
students as we had facilities for. Our class of 1949
numbered four hundred and ninety-one—the largest class
ever graduated, before or since, from any school of
journalism.

A pair of bright young men were sent out to Columbia
by *Collier's* in 1957 to "do" an article about our school
for that magazine. They were so impressed by the size
of our student body that they wrote their piece mainly on
the theme of the large number of reporters the *Missourian*
used for its news coverage of Columbia—two for every
block within the city limits, they imagined! It was not
mere "coverage," they said, but "blanketing"; and they
entitled their article "The City Without Secrets." It was
clever, and the kind of fanciful piece that suited *Collier's*
in those years when it was starting its long toboggan-
slide to oblivion; but we did not like it very well, probably
because there was some unpalatable truth in it. We did
have so many reporters that we usually had to assign
several to a single event and send others seeking and
searching for crumbs of news. Perhaps that was not bad,
but too many students rarely saw anything they wrote in
print.

I have said that these were harried months, but they
were in many ways happy and rewarding. We found the
returned GI's generally good students. Most of them
appreciated our efforts to expand as much and as fast as
we could and co-operated sincerely and constructively.
I do not regard the statistics of that big class of '49 with
any spirit of boastfulness, however; I shall always regret

that classes were for a few years too large to permit the
school to do all that it might have done for its students
in classrooms less crowded and laboratories less over-
worked.

That brings us squarely up to the key question: what
should a school of journalism do for its students? Fore-
most in the minds of the teachers and administrators of
the schools, departments, colleges, institutes, etc., of
journalism and communications, as they are variously
called nowadays throughout the country, is the fundamental problem of the proper aims and principles of
education in this field. But before I set forth a brief
"creed" embodying what I believe to be the thinking of
our leaders on that question, I must interpose here one
sweeping disclaimer.

A college education is certainly not necessary for
success in journalism. From Benjamin Franklin, who
was "put to school" for only two years, down to certain
leaders in the newspaper profession today who have never
had much formal education, I could make a long list of
great editors and publishers who never had the experience
of a college discipline. You cannot wrap up human
nature in a syllogism, or put bounds to genius, or tell
what industry or aptitude or luck will do for a man. By
the same token, it would be absurd to claim that a course
in a journalism school is either a necessity or a guarantee
of success in the communications field. The fact is that
a copyboy can still sometimes work his way to top
management without even a high school education, and
a college graduate who has had no guidance from a
journalism school and is totally ignorant of newspaper
processes can frequently find a good job and make a
brilliant success in journalism.

In other words, much may be claimed for self-education. A strong, independent character may go far on his own industry and talent; but it is, at best, a risky business. It is a trial-and-error system. The value of a more formal education is found largely in the student's subjection to a rigorous discipline which is founded upon the long experience, the continuous study, and the careful decisions of a faculty and administration that devote their lives to forming that discipline. The student finds himself within a pattern of working, playing, living, and thinking that is designed to call up his best resources, his full powers. Full allowance is made for the aptitudes and aims of the individual student, of course, but compliance with a wisely-designed system is essential in formal education.

I believe there is substantial agreement among leaders in education for journalism today on the philosophy, or principles, governing their own discipline; and I shall try to set it all out here in four articles of a "creed."

ONE. The student must be well grounded in the humanities, the social sciences, and the natural sciences. There is no profession that makes demands upon a more various knowledge than does journalism. The handling of the news of the complex and confused world of today is an appalling responsibility, and it requires the resources of a mind that has, at the least, adventured in many fields. Moreover, the liberal subjects condition the student for a richer enjoyment of life, and that is one of the chief aims of any good education.

A caution is in order here. Let us beware of attaching the tag "liberal" to certain subjects, and to others, by implication, that of "illiberal." My friend Francis Horn observed a few years ago upon his inauguration as president of Pratt Institute: "The fact is that no subject, of itself, is liberal. It is not *what* the student studies that gives him a liberal education, but *how* he studies it, and the way it is taught. Just as the so-called liberal subjects can be taught illiberally, likewise so-called vocational subjects can and should be taught liberally." I always thought of my own lectures in "History and Principles of Journalism" as a liberal course despite the technical word in the title, and the same may be said of many other courses labeled "Journalism."

But regardless of the essential liberalism of various studies, it is the general agreement in our field that the journalism major should take about three-fourths of his work in the colleges of arts and sciences, depending somewhat on whether his course extends over four or five years.

TWO. The student must also receive instruction in the practices and techniques of the various phases of journalism. This specialized training, conducted by teachers with adequate professional backgrounds, makes use of laboratory facilities varying greatly in the different schools. A campus newspaper is common, and internships or other on-the-job types of work in nearby co-operating papers are used by some schools.

Training to know and training to make use of what one knows are properly two parts of one process. It is my own conviction, based on many years of observation of student experience, that the combination of learning and doing, theory and technique, analysis and creation often does more to liberate the mind and spirit of youth than endless hours of listening to lectures in classrooms and reading assignments in libraries.

Alfred North Whitehead once stated the whole matter very well. "What we should aim at producing," he wrote, "is men who possess both culture and expert knowledge in some special direction. Their expert knowledge will give them the ground to start from, and their culture will lead them as deep as philosophy and as high as art."

THREE. The student must follow a prescribed curriculum. This usually has some rigid requirements, as in history, science, writing, and the languages; but it provides great latitude, with sympathetic and knowledgeable guidance, for the student aiming at a specific kind of job. Work in communications becomes more and more specialized in our era. The old-time managing editor who figured that his boys were all reporters together and anyone could cover a science story, a philharmonic concert, or an ecumenical conference tends to become a ridiculous figure—at least on a metropolitan paper. And the electronic media, advertising in its myriad phases, readership analysis, magazine work, and photojournalism call for the development of specific skills. Thus the student will commonly do some specializing; but, on the other hand, he has to be so advised that he may take advantage of the richness and variety afforded by the whole university. If he can spend five years with us instead of four, so much the better are his chances for a really liberal education. For all this, he needs both rules and informed advisement.

Many do not realize how much study and experimentation is carried on throughout the years by educators in the effort to determine what integrations of the liberal arts and the natural sciences, of required and elective courses, of study and performance, and the like will be most effective for the direction and training that will lead to a successful professional career, and, at the same time, to the general culture that makes life worth living. This is a major factor in the service rendered by a good school of journalism.

FOUR. The student must be exposed to a climate of

respect for journalism and loyalty to its ideals. We are not training hucksters. Through courses in the history of journalism, ethics, sociology, psychology, etc., we invite thinking about our profession in relation to primary categories and on a high level. The advancement of journalism along professional lines in the past fifty years has been due largely to the schools, and ethical standards of the future will be set mainly by our graduates.

. . . So this is our "creed." This is what we are trying to do. I used to think it was better not to say or write much about what we were doing, except in our functional school announcements, because we were sure to get mixed up in bitter debates with our critics. It was better, I thought, to keep on doing the best job we could and let our work speak for us. Well, our graduates now speak for us in many quarters. I suppose we have "infiltrated the enemy." At any rate, things have changed. Our own convention programs used to be filled with reports made up from answers to questionnaires as to how managing editors were regarding us—mostly with disfavor, it seemed. I note that the Associated Press Managing Editors' group headed its program not long ago with a report on research as to why the newspapers were not getting their share of the output of schools of journalism.

Not that the ancient flood of objection to education for journalism has entirely subsided. I wish what we have of it today were all founded on careful study and observation of what we are actually doing, so that we might really benefit by it. But most informed criticism seems to come from within our own group, where it is lively and useful, and scarcely any of those who attack us in an occasional piece in a magazine or in a newspaper editorial have, I am afraid, improved their standing over what it was in Pulitzer's day, when that great editor called critics of his plan "prejudiced and ignorant." There seem to be two classes of censors, as they have come to my attention in recent years. There is the old chap (sometimes not so old) who has not himself been through the educational discipline but has known a journalism graduate or teacher whom he did not approve, and so condemns the whole movement out of hand without knowing much about it. Then there is the carper somewhere in the periphery of the educational field who has an axe to grind; he knows little about schools of journalism and wants to know less. These types are sorry remnants of the army of forthright critics once led by Greeley and Watterson and Godkin.

Today a large proportion of the colleges and universities of the United States offer at least a course or two in journalism. Latest additions to the list, as I write these lines, are Princeton University, with its new Ferris Professorship of Journalism and Public Relations, and the Annenberg School of Communications at the University of Pennsylvania. There is great diversity in all this instruction in the wide communications field. At the last count of which I am aware, more than a hundred and thirty institutions offered what they called "full professional training in journalism." At the beginning of the 1960's, forty-eight "schools" or other units had been accredited by the American Council on Education for Journalism, which operates as a joint committee of educators and professional journalists. Accreditation means that, in the opinion of the visiting examiners, a school offers one or more acceptable "sequences" in the field, providing an adequate faculty, library, and laboratory, in co-operation with an approved arts and science program.

It is, of course, gratifying to realize that journalism has been accepted so generally as one of the disciplines in our American system of higher education; but, on the other hand, some of the statistics I have just recited are nothing less than appalling. Nobody can ponder them without realizing that there must be a vast deal of amateurish, time-wasting course work going on under the name of education for journalism. One of the best thinkers on the problems of our field called not long ago for a "drastic reduction" in the number of units of journalism instruction in American colleges and universities, but nobody has drastically reduced anything in these inflationary years. Obviously, reduction in quantity should be based on criteria of quality; but refusal to accredit simply does not work (thus far, at least) as a reducing instrumentality, and what will? I have no method to suggest for arbitrarily closing what some of us may believe to be the inferior units in a field like communications, in which freedom to proliferate is connected (ideologically, if not legally) with the constitutional guarantee of the freedom of the press. The way to improvement will continue to be, as it has been in the past, a long and hard road to follow.

The number of units clearly has some bearing, in actual practice, on the problem of quality; the size of the units probably has little relationship to it. I know some schools that do very well with limited programs.

It is heartening, however, to look back upon the progress of education for journalism during the years in which I have observed its developing pattern. In the better schools, at least, it is today a much more respectable scholarly discipline than it was only two or three decades ago. Instruction, laboratories, and buildings are improved almost beyond recognition.

Who were the boys who were active in this movement, its leaders, in the thick of its fights? I find it natural to call them "boys" because they were young fellows when I first knew them—though some are now tagged with the somewhat equivocal title, "emeritus." I wish to name three or four. Many of us (and I especially) have owed much to Ralph D. Casey, who gathered such a stimulating faculty about him at Minnesota. In the thirties I used to make an annual pilgrimage to Minneapolis on one excuse or another but mainly to keep in touch with Casey and his crew. Ralph O. Nafziger was for years on Casey's faculty but later resigned to direct with notable success the journalism work at Wisconsin. Kenneth E. Olson was for some time also a member of that group; later he was dean of Northwestern and active in the accreditation program. Also active in that movement were two men who, fortunately for journalism education, are well short of retirement age as I write these pages—Earl F. English and Norval Neil Luxon. English came to us at Iowa with the record of a notable success in high school journalism; he became an ill-paid member of my staff while he was undergoing the severe discipline of our psychologists that eventually led to a doctorate in that department, and later he joined us at Missouri. We loaned him to the Accrediting Committee for a year or two, and he worked out brilliantly the pioneer techniques of that difficult operation; later he succeeded (and, I may as well confess, exceeded) me in his imaginative and indefatigable conduct of the varied and comprehensive activities involved in the deanship of the Missouri School of Journalism. Luxon, who left administrative work at Ohio State to become dean of the Journalism School at North Carolina, was also a wheel-horse in the early accreditation work and continues a fearless and outspoken advocate of the highest standards in our field.

I am reminded of an incident that occurred during

my early years at Iowa. As an English professor, I was asked to write a story about a drama department production of "As You Like It" for the student newspaper. I thought it an excellent amateur performance and wrote in glowing terms of nearly everyone in the cast, from Rosalind to Touchstone. Bruce Gould, later co-editor with his wife of the *Ladies' Home Journal*, was running a clever editorial-page column in the paper at the time headed "Chills and Fever"; he noticed the production, too, and observed that in his newspaper critique "Mott kissed them all 'round."

It would be absurd for me to try to catalogue here all of my old friends and yoke-fellows in what we regarded as a kind of crusade for the advancement of education for journalism through some thirty or forty years. But I think I must name Chilton R. Bush, out at Stanford; Wilbur Schramm, the brilliant writer and scholar who followed me at Iowa and is now also at Stanford; Raymond B. Nixon, editor of the *Journalism Quarterly* and a leader in the internationalization of journalistic studies; the versatile Roscoe Ellard, once of Missouri and later of Columbia; Frederick S. Siebert, authority on law of the press, whom I knew best during his long term as head of the School at Illinois; Lawrence W. Murphy, who preceded him in that post; Jerry O'Sullivan, beloved dean of the School at Marquette; H. H. Herbert, of Oklahoma; John E. Drewry, of Georgia. . . . Indeed, I omit from this testament of regard the names of some of those I have liked best and valued most. A grand group of scholars, gentlemen, great teachers, devoted leaders in the improvement of education for journalism.

And now I see a new group coming forward, with new ideas, new points of view, a broadening culture and understanding of the world today. On every hand, concepts and techniques are developing, others newly appearing, still others just over the horizon. Perhaps we cannot see it today, but may we not tomorrow be on the verge of a revolution in education for journalism that will be an integral part of a revolution in mass communication? Our field extends itself before us with endless varieties of electronic offerings, shifting problems of mass media and mass culture, the application of new statistical and psychological principles to all phases of communication, the active forward march of photojournalism in both techniques and ideology, the constantly developing science and philosophy of semantics, the concerted attack upon the vital problems of the economics of publishing, the revolutionary progress in the mechanics of composition and printing. . . .

11

Unfinished Story; or, The Man in the Carrel

THIS IS THE STORY OF A PROJECT. It is the unfinished story of something that began in a boyish enthusiasm, developed over a term of years into what may be fairly called "a large undertaking," and eventually became a lifetime work. This is how it all came about.

Country editors in the 1890's could receive all the magazines they wanted free, provided they inserted in their weekly papers little excerpts from the current issues, usually with tag-lines telling about how interesting *Harper's* or *McClure's* was that month. These were attractive "fillers" and also good advertising for the magazines.

Throughout his long career as editor of weekly papers, my father took advantage of this exchange arrangement with many good magazines. Since we never threw any of them away, they accumulated in piles and dusty heaps. Thus the roomy closet of the upstairs room assigned to my brother and me came to be filled with old copies of *Harper's, Scribner's, Century, Atlantic, Review of Reviews, McClure's, Cosmopolitan, Chautauquan, St. Nicholas,* and so on. These old magazines were a source of endless pleasure to me on Sunday afternoons, rainy days, and many long evenings. Am I wrong in thinking that the stories, essays, and poems in those old pages were really ambrosial fare? Or have they been transformed from something very ordinary by the magic of my fond recollection? No; as I have thumbed through them in recent years, looking at pictures by the "high society" Charles Dana Gibson, the romantic Howard Pyle, the humorous A. B. Frost, and others, including the matchless engravings of old masters by Timothy Cole, and rereading Kipling and Hardy, Howells and Garland, and T. R. and Carnegie and Tarbell—I still find that the nineties seem to me a golden age in our periodical literature.

Certainly those magazines were precious to me when I pored over them in my boyhood. Moreover, it seemed shameful to allow them to lie in their sterile stacks there in our closet. So I arranged them in proper files and then set out to index them. I had never heard of *Poole's Index*, or of the newer *Readers' Guide to Periodical Literature;* I was thinking only of making the treasures I had at hand more accessible for a rather indeterminate use in a vague future. My father had discarded a big ledger after brief use of it in one of his less successful side-ventures in business, and its empty pages were just what I needed. Mine was an author-title index. I worked on it pretty faithfully in my spare hours for the better part of a year, as I recall—until other activities diverted my attention. Occasionally thereafter I came back to it to index a few numbers of the beautiful and superior *Scribner's* of the nineties, or the old John Brisben Walker *Cosmopolitan*, with the broad red band up and down the left side of its cover.

My parents did not quite approve of this too sedentary, ink-horn occupation of mine, but they did not forbid it. I stuck to it through a kind of compulsion that I am not psychologist enough to explain. Boyhood is always subject to brief zealotries and manias, which sometimes have important effects on later life. My indexing experience tended to systematize my liking for old magazines—to put it on paper, as it were, and give it a kind of permanence. The names of the great magazinists were like a chime of bells in my memory—Brownell, Boyesen, Garland, Hardy, Howells, Kipling, Stevenson, Stockton. . . .

And so, years later, when Professor Trent, at Columbia University, asked me what topic I wished to explore in a doctoral dissertation, I suggested a historical essay on the *Galaxy*, and he warmly approved. The *Galaxy* was a New York magazine distinguished by the contributions of Henry James, Mark Twain, and Walt Whitman. Begun in 1866, it was merged twelve years later with the *Atlantic Monthly*. But I soon found that the story of the *Galaxy* and its editors and contributors was only part of the closely-woven pattern of the history of American periodicals in the decade or two following the Civil War; and before I realized it, my plan had broadened and I was writing about the whole output of magazines and journals and their various trends and phases during that active and yeasty post-bellum period.

Long before this study was finished, however, I had become disturbingly conscious of the fact that the roots of the publishing and editorial movements of the period I was examining were deep in the preceding years, and also what I saw developing in the seventies was to continue with greater momentum and clearer meaning in the eighties and nineties. In the concluding paragraph of my dissertation, I declared that the years I had been studying comprised a transition period; but I have since learned that all historical "periods" are transitional, each of them not only displaying the effects of causes discernible in times that have gone before but also containing the seeds of things that may flower in times to come. As an idea, this may seem obvious and unexciting; but as a practical, working situation, based on an array of facts, it was dynamic and revolutionary in my own plans for study and writing.

What I then resolved to do was to write a comprehensive history of American magazines from the beginnings by Franklin and Bradford down to the present—and to include in the term "magazines" the journals, reviews, periodicals, and all the salmagundi of serials that were not actually newspapers. I have often thought that a more suitable title for my work would be "A History of American Periodicals." But when I took the project to academic advisers and publishers, it was "A History of American Magazines," and the title stuck, and so it is, for better or worse.

I must say that not all of those academic advisers looked with favor on my project. One very great scholar shook his grey head gravely and told me that two lifetimes would not be enough to do what I contemplated. Others here and there (and I canvassed opinions widely) were also skeptical. But when I took these discouraging verdicts to Thomas A. Knott, himself as great a scholar as any of them, he removed the corncob pipe from between his teeth and asked, "You really want to do this, don't you?"

"That I do," I replied.

Knott took one of those big kitchen matches that he carried about with him from his pocket and lit his pipe; and when he had taken a puff or two, took the pipe out of his mouth, blew out a cloud of smoke, grinned, and said: "Go ahead!"

With men like Craig and Knott at Iowa and Trent and

Van Doren at Columbia believing in me, it was easier to buckle down to work. And support soon came from another quarter. Francis G. Wickware was a Canadian-born mining engineer who had early turned to academic and literary pursuits and was, when I knew him, the suave and scholarly editor for D. Appleton and Company. He became interested in my project, and in due time I had a contract for the publication of the first volume of my history.

Perhaps the very great scholar who was once my adviser had a clearer understanding of the difficulties of the task I had set myself than I did. I have sometimes thought he was right about his "two lifetimes." I had a full academic load of teaching and administration, and my writing and research had to be done at night and on week ends and holidays. The "I Led Three Lives" chap on television had nothing on me: I led one life in classroom and office, one in libraries and at my typewriter, and a third as a family man and a social being of sorts. I am not complaining; I loved it.

My family never failed in sympathy and helpfulness. When the time came to make an index for the first volume, my wife and our daughter Mildred and I locked the doors of our house, answered no telephone calls, and lived on canned soup, sandwiches, and coffee until the job was done. My wife and daughter accompanied me on visits to great libraries: we once made a family junket of a tour of eastern repositories, moving into a Worcester apartment while I was at work in the American Antiquarian Society collection, and living for a while in Concord while I communted to Boston to dig in the Boston Public Library and that of the Massachusetts Historical Society. Later, when Mildred was a graduate student in archeolo-

gy at the University of Chicago, we made trips to the
Newberry and Crerar occasions for family reunions.

When the second volume was ready for the press, I
had publisher trouble. Appleton had been impatient for
it; but it was not finished until the years of the great depression were upon us, bringing with them embarrass-
ments for that publishing house. The first volume had
done well enough in sales; but quick-moving titles were
now considered imperative by the bankers of the D.
Appleton-Century Company, which was soon to become
D. Appleton-Century-Crofts. They might be able to
take my book in a year or two, but if I did not want to
wait. . . . I did not, and soon had the manuscript back
on my hands. I queried other publishers; but I was now
in the position of trying to place the second volume of a
series that the publishers of the first volume had rejected,
and all were wary. They were more than wary; they
were unanimously uninterested. Eventually the Modern
Language Association set up a committee to read my
manuscript and report on its acceptability for issue by
means of the organization's Revolving Book Publication
Fund. But when the three scholars had waded through
the two thousand typed pages and had agreed to recommend publication, it was discovered that the Revolving
Fund had no funds in it to set it revolving any more—or
at least not for some time. Then it was that the incisive,
ever-helpful Howard Mumford Jones, who had just joined
the Harvard faculty and who had been a member of the
M.L.A. committee that had read my manuscript, wrote me
that this thing must be published and that he was taking
the matter up with Dumas Malone, the new director of a
rejuvenated Harvard University Press. This made the
beginning of a happy connection with a publishing house
that has been as tolerant and forbearing as any author

could wish. In 1938 it brought out under its own imprint the first three hefty volumes of my history.

There were some protests (rather amused and mild ones, I think) over the publication of a work carrying some very rude and raucous material by this decorous press. They were apparently called forth largely by Malone's impish insertion in the fall announcement of the press of an illustration from my second volume showing a scandalous cover page from the *Police Gazette.* Out in St. Louis the *Post-Dispatch* carried an editorial entitled "An Eyebrow-Raiser," which I have since learned was written by Irving Dilliard, and which is amusing enough to reprint here:

Things must be in a pretty way in old Cambridge as the brown leaves float down through these October afternoons from the arching elms in Harvard Yard. It is the "Autumn Announcement" of the Harvard University Press, 38 Quincy St., hard by President Conant's house, which gives cause for the alarm.

For the Harvard University Press is a dignified adjunct of our oldest institution of learning, presided over by the scholarly Dr. Dumas Malone, lately editor of the monumental "Dictionary of American Biography." Its publications are sizable tomes on such things as prehistoric remains, Indo-Iranian languages, early Greek elegists, boundary conflicts in South America, Chinese historiography, time budgets of human behavior, the physiocratic doctrine of judicial control, and the old Frisian Skeltana-Riucht.

And yet the first illustration in the current catalogue to fall beneath our eye was of deepest saffron. Two buxom dames of the hour-glass school of feminine charms are presented as entertaining two heavily-mustached, silk-hatted gentlemen in a lavish chamber. The blonde is reclining on a royal couch, while the brunette perches on the knee of the other guest, an endearing arm about his neck. Champagne bottles are in evidence and tell-tale goblets in air. The caption: "A masher mashed—How a Chicago youth of the 'too awfully sweet for anything' variety, while essaying the role of a lady killer, was taken in and done for, like the veriest countryman, by a brace of sharp damsels and their male accomplice. See page 7."

And then we found that we were looking at the cover of the *Police Gazette* for July 26, 1876, reproduced as an illustration from Frank Luther Mott's three-volume "History of American Magazines," which the Harvard Press is issuing this fall!

Let the editor and his cohorts defend their illustration on the score of historical scholarship if they will. Just wait until they hear from the teacups that tinkle across the blue Charles in prim and proper Back Bay!

The *Harvard Alumni Bulletin* further reported that some private letters to the press had commented on the fact that "this reprehensible illustration from the naughty Seventies" appeared on the verso of a reproduction of a portrait of Oliver Wendell Holmes which was being used as the frontispiece of Felix Frankfurter's *Mr. Justice Holmes and the Supreme Court,* also announced for publication that fall. "To pained protestors against the indignity to the revered Justice," observed the editor of the *Bulletin,* "the reply has been made that he himself would undoubtedly be tickled to find the *Police Gazette* on his august back."

Such publicity, I assume, did not injure the sale of the books. Deeply aware of the faults and shortcomings of my work, I awaited the reviews with trepidation. I have always envied those authors who say they never read reviews of their books, and have wondered why, when they do not read the criticisms, they rail so fiercely at the critics. But the reviewers—both those who have really read the books and those who have only thumbed through them—have nearly always been more than kind to me. Thus publishing troubles, crowded schedules, the expense of travel to distant repositories, and the occasional laborious searching, enumerating, and recording of the contents of the great directories and catalogs—all of this at last began to seem like a tale of harrowing adventure turning out well in the end. Then came the satisfaction of a Pulitzer Prize for the second and third volumes, and later a Bancroft Prize, even more rewarding both in sentimental value and in cash, awarded by Columbia University to the fourth volume. Nor was I unappreciative of recognition by Sigma Delta Chi and Kappa Tau Alpha. And so I have been heartened to go on in my later years with the fifth and sixth volumes.

I do not wish to imply that I have found my labor on these big books generally irksome. Quite the contrary. A great deal of it has been tedious and tiresome, indeed; but on the whole, the essential fascination of the task has remained fresh and strong enough throughout the years to make the work continuously enjoyable.

A great library has always been to me a kind of minor heaven, and its librarians angels in disguise. Sometimes a very dusty, ill-ventilated and ill-lighted heaven, to be sure, with its angels carefully concealing their wings. There may seem to be no end of monkey-like climbing of winding iron stairs, ramps, and runways in the great bookstacks; of lifting heavy volumes from high shelves and blowing the dust off them; of hunting comfortable, lighted desks and tables on which to work—but there is nevertheless a feeling of romantic adventure about it all and, more than that, a kind of satisfaction and contentment in the midst of such rich treasures.

Yet I see a certain irony in the figure of a lone researcher working in the stacks of a great library. I remember one of those "fillers" with which Mencken and Nathan used to stop up chinks in pages of the old *Smart Set*. I cannot find it now, but it ran somewhat like this:

A man sits at a small desk in a carrel in the midst of the bookstacks of a great library. All about him tower the high shelves—mountains of books with little iron paths running high up along their sides. Thousands, millions of books, bound in cracked calfskin, faded cloth, stout buckram. Serried row on row of books in battalions and armies—ancient, medieval, modern—fat and thin, tall and short. Multitudes of dusty books towering above and about the man in the carrel. What is the man doing? He is writing a book.

They may laugh at the men in the carrels, and we may laugh at ourselves; but we continue to dig away, and to enjoy it, and to hope that the results may, in some strange way, justify our activities. I have spent many happy hours among the treasures that lie behind the small green door of the library of the American Antiquarian Society in Worcester, Massachusetts. For months and years I had a passing acquaintance with the stone lions that guard the great edifice at Fifth Avenue and Forty-second Street in New York. I have invaded many of the cloistered repositories of books held by the older historical societies in the East, as well as less formally guarded collections in the Midwest. The AP-2 stacks of the Library of Congress have been a second home to me through sweltering summer months as well as weeks of winter cold. I knew the L.C. when its Rare Book Room was a littered, airless attic, and when many magazine files were shelved along dark corridors; now the Rare Book Room is a place of light and joy, with controlled temperature and humidity, and the class periodicals are also to be found in the great air-conditioned annex.

I have spent long days and evenings in Chicago's Newberry Library, where I found the shelves richly laden and the staff helpful; and when its doors closed at night I would hurry down North Clark Street's "skid row," illuminated mainly by bursts of light from cheap night-clubs, on the half-hour walk to my hotel. In the John Crerar Library, then in the Chicago Loop but now soon to be moved, I found exciting files of rare technical journals. The Iowa State Library in Des Moines formerly possessed a surprising abundance of files of old magazines, and the officials there would allow me to work in its stacks all alone at nights and on Sundays when I would run away from Iowa City over week ends and holidays. Perhaps I owe most of all to the great university libraries at Iowa, Missouri, Wisconsin, Columbia, Pennsylvania, Western Reserve, Northwestern, and Harper Memorial at Chicago. I have worked, too, from time to time in some of the great city libraries; New York's I have mentioned, but I have vivid memories too of those in Boston, Chicago, and St. Louis. All these I list out of sheer gratitude and could name many more. Few libraries have seemed to me unfriendly; few librarians have seemed reluctant to afford all the help that could reasonably be asked by the man in the carrel.

Long ago I set up a time-and-work program that called for finishing my magazine project in 1950. What has chiefly prevented such a consummation has been the interruption of my schedule by other writing tasks that have forced themselves (or so it seemed) upon me from time to time—a history of American newspapers, a history of best sellers in the United States, an expository and descriptive book on news and how it is handled in the United States for the "Library of Congress Series in American Civilization," a study of Jefferson and his relations with the press, annual collections of best news stories in the thirties, and other books I have wanted to write or, in some cases, to edit. Then there were extensive contributions to the *Britannica* and some to several other encyclopedias, many book reviews, some work for USIS, occasional more or less scholarly papers, and even some short stories. Many of these books and articles have been rather closely connected with my magazine undertaking; but, after all, they were diversionary. A more single-minded dedication to a fixed goal would have brought my chief work to completion on schedule. Yet I have always returned faithfully—after other "pursuits and excursions"—to the magazine study, as I shall return to it again after this little book is finished. As the errant lover in Ernest Dowson's poem protested, "I have been faithful to thee, Cynara! in my fashion."

I should be unhappy if, by devoting as much space as I have here given to one man's experience in a big research-and-writing project, I should leave any reader with the thought that I consider these books of mine to be history on the grand scale. There are many kinds of historical writing. There is, for example, what I am wont to think of as "grand history," which deals with epic movements of peoples or elucidates the meaning of a series of great events. But, among the various types, there is also a humble kind of history that Moses Hadas recently called "ancilla," and Justin Winsor once referred to (in describing his own work) as "shreds-and-patches history." This is the category in which my work belongs —though I am encouraged to think that I have, here and there, helped to define patterns of thought (and sometimes lack of thought) in the American past.

And I do hope yet to see all six fat volumes of my *History of American Magazines,* in their handsome Belknap Press bindings, on my shelves. If not, however, I shall never complain that I have not found time enough; but I shall confess frankly that my dereliction has been due to finding, through the years of my life, too many allurements in too many projects, all of them tempting me from the straiter path.

12

Biarritz American University

WE WERE A MOTLEY CREW. There were two hundred and fifty of us—assorted professors from a hundred colleges and universities all over the United States. We had been invited by the United States Army to join in a unique educational project.

About two-thirds of us left New York early on the morning after Independence Day of 1945, on the "Queen Elizabeth," and the remainder came along a few days later on the "Queen Mary." We sailed just two months after V-E Day. When the fighting ended, there were some two and a half million American soldiers in the European Theater of Operations, and virtually all of them were desperately impatient to get home. Obviously, it would take a long time to transfer to the United States the troops designed for demobilization. It was a bad experience for those hundreds of thousands—millions—of boys to have to wait for transport home; and the "points" given each man in the attempt to equate service with priority of shipment did little to alleviate the acute pains of delay and postponement and waiting. I once visited the great staging area of Calais, near Marseilles, where hundreds of thousands of our boys were encamped for longer or shorter periods while awaiting sailings from that port; and I was impressed by the entertainments provided for the waiting men by the army's special services. But I think that all the GI's who were ever encamped there unanimously hated Calais for what they had to undergo in that installation. I am sure that for many of these boys combat duty was more acceptable than "sweating out" the boat home.

The army, which must always be foresighted, gave attention to the prospect of such a situation long before it developed, planning not only entertainment features but serious educational projects to occupy the attention of the men awaiting demobilization. This program included the stepping up of the work which had been conducted by the army unit schools, staffed by officers and dealing mainly with technical subjects; increases in the work of the Armed Forces Institute, the great correspondence school with which home universities had long co-operated; and even the establishment of a centralized technological center at Florence, Italy. But the biggest and most striking educational undertaking in the program was the founding of two full-scale army universities with faculties drawn both from the military forces then in Europe and from what was sometimes called, in official jargon, the Zone of the Interior. One of these institutions was to be located in England and the other in France, and it was for them that our crew had been brought together.

I heard no little talk from time to time about who "dreamed up" the idea of army universities. Doubtless a search of official papers would reveal the names of those who first showed a decisive interest in such a project. Top officers of the Information and Education Division were, of course, largely responsible. General Paul H. Thompson, head of I. and E., certainly deserved much credit. One of the first to urge the idea was Colonel Paul

C. Packer, on leave from the State University of Iowa as an adviser to the Special Services Division. But whoever dreamed it up, it was approved shortly after V-E Day and preparations began with a rush.

The task was tremendous. It was planned to assemble at the two centers top-rating faculties, adequate libraries, and the necessary laboratory equipment and teaching facilities for large universities; to transport to each of these centers on a given date thousands of selected GI students, register them for courses, and provide quarters, messes, and living arrangements for them; and to find suitable sites and buildings for classes, offices, and quarters—and to bring everything together in order and begin sessions in ten weeks' time. The whole operation still seems to me an extraordinary accomplishment—a prodigy of drive and integrated effort.

As soon as the War Department approved the project, a group of faculty recruiters headed by Dean Packer was assembled at the Pentagon in Washington. At least twenty persons worked for long or shorter "tours of duty" at this business of getting together a faculty for the two overseas universities. I worked with the group for about a week and found that its members had been chosen because of their wide acquaintance with educational personnel the country over. We accepted no applications directly from candidates; we initiated our own inquiries and did much talking over long-distance telephones as we looked into the qualifications of various men suggested. We wanted, first of all, good teachers, and second, men who would be co-operative in situations that might be difficult. We were glad to get distinguished scholars when we could; but even more we wanted men of force and character, men who would be resourceful in an educational adventure. When we sailed, we thought that our group represented those qualities; and, with a few exceptions, our two faculties performed services of a notably high character.

The crossing on the "Queen Elizabeth" was smooth and pleasant. Eight men in one stateroom made up in sociability what they lacked in conveniences. We were told that on its westward voyage the week before, the "Elizabeth" had carried sixteen thousand passengers and crew, and there had been thirty-two men assigned to our stateroom, with staggered sleeping periods. A steward told me that two months earlier, whenever the ship was at sea all passengers had to wear life belts whenever they came on deck. If a steward caught sight of a man who was not obeying the rule, it was his duty to send him back to his cabin after the necessary article and to hold one of his shoes as surety for his return properly equipped. My English steward was still enjoying that experience in retrospect. "It was rare sport," he said, "to walk up to a brigadier and ask, 'May I have your shoe, sir?'"

We anchored in the Firth of Clyde and went ashore at Greenock, Scotland, to take a train south. At Southampton we parted from our friends who were assigned to the English university, while we Frenchmen took a Channel boat that was crowded to the point of standing room only. I slept with five hundred other men in a section of the hold where bunks were piled five high. Not all the smells came from the sleepers, for the garbage cans were located at the bottom of the companionway of our bunkroom. But it was a short passage and a smooth one, and the morning was enlivened by the sport of shooting at floating mines by the ship's gun. Our gunner made a pretty bad score.

During our ten days in Paris, we were lodged at the *Cité Universitaire*. It was a happy time. We did some sightseeing, for this was, for some of us, a first visit to Paris: but our waking hours were mainly occupied with getting acquainted with our military environment and developing plans for our great educational experiment.

When a United States Army university in France had first been suggested, the idea had been to set it up at Fontainebleau, and a site near Paris would have had its advantages; but by the time of our arrival, Biarritz, on the Bay of Biscay, had been fixed upon. This famous watering-place had been a favorite with wealthy Europeans ever since the Empress Eugénie had made it popular in the middle of the last century. With its luxury hotels, its many fine villas, and its peerless beach, it was a marvelous site for our university.

But our English friends opened their school three weeks before the one in France. Shrivenham, in the Thames valley some sixty miles west of London and twenty miles southwest of Oxford, required less changing and adaptation to fit it to educational purposes than did Biarritz. At Shrivenham there had been a kind of annex to the Royal Military College at Sandhurst, not far away. The buildings were therefore well suited to use as classrooms, offices, and lodgings; and the grounds were as beautiful as those of Sandhurst itself. I visited Shrivenham American University when it was in mid-career, and its green lawns and grand old trees made me think of Constable landscapes. Dean Kenneth E. Olson, on leave from Northwestern University, who had been a consultant on the over-all project from an early date, was chief of the journalism section at Shrivenham.

Ten days before Shrivenham opened, our group changed its base to Biarritz. On the evening of July 19, we took one of those long and unbelievably crowded wartime trains south out of Paris. There was very little sleep for anyone that night, but we did our best to make a lark of it. We had breakfast during a long stop at Bordeaux, where French Red Cross girls met us with sandwiches made of thick slices of grey bread and grape jelly, and pitchers of *vin ordinaire*.

When we first arrived in Biarritz, most of us were lodged in the world-famous Hôtel Miramar; later we found quarters here and there in the pleasant villas with which the resort city abounds. Schools and departments of the university generally made their homes in these large residences, most of which had recently been occupied by departments of the German occupation forces. The Villa Rochefoucauld, once a favorite holiday residence of Queen Victoria, became our fine arts building. The municipal casino was transformed into a university library, the gaming tables being moved aside to make room for bookshelves and reading desks. The headquarters of General Samuel L. McCroskey, commandant of the whole university installation, were in the Napoleon suite of the Hôtel du Palais, the magnificent hostelry erected by Napoleon III for Empress Eugénie. And I may say that at the Palais there was a mess which was something rather special. A mess? Rather *un palais de la cuisine*.

Rentals for the university and many of its supplies cost American taxpayers nothing directly, since they represented French returns on American loans—what was known as "reverse lend-lease." The hotels were empty except for skeleton staffs, because during this crisis there were few people actually vacationing at European resorts. The villas had been deserted by their owners upon the German occupation and they were usually easy to obtain for our uses. One of the difficulties of life in Biarritz in the winter of 1945-46 came from the fact that facilities for *chauffage central* had fallen into disuse, boilers had rusted out, and so on. Besides, coal was a scarce commodity in Europe then. And southwestern France can get very cold in the winter months.

Some of the initial shortcomings in supplies were bad enough. Our two crucial shortages on opening day were books and chairs. Lists of books had been made and orders placed (or we thought they had been placed) for many volumes before we left the States, but all through the first term the supply of books was painfully inadequate. We never did have enough chairs for classrooms and lecture halls, but the boys improvised benches or sat on the floor when necessary. Among the items requisitioned for the university that I remember as making special trouble were twenty-five pianos for the music department, a herd of cows for the dairy department, and ten tons of print paper in rolls cut tabloid size for our journalism school's newspaper. The need was too pressing to allow time to obtain materials from home; even most of the books with which we began instruction we had to find in E.T.O. But with the power of the United States Army behind us, and with a large amount of skillful "scrounging," we brought the necesary supplies together.

Up to the night before the day set for the beginning of registration, no students had arrived. Transport delays had held them up at various points in western Europe. Faculty had vacated the big hotels in their favor because, first, there was a strong feeling that since these boys had been having it very rough for a long time, they deserved a spot of luxury now; and, second, it was believed that lodging students in large dormitories had many advantages over scattering them throughout the city. And the students did get there, most of them on time. In the middle of the night before that first registration day, a long train crowded and jammed with tired, hungry GI's pulled into the Biarritz station. They marched up Boulevard Edouard Sept (which they were later to call the "Main Drag"), and when they came in sight of the great Hôtel Miramar, in which they were to be quartered, they burst into loud cheering all along the line. Biarrotes turned on their pillows and asked sleepily, "*Qu'est ce que c'est?*" After a moment's listening had reassured them that the Germans had not returned, they said, "*Alors, les Americains arrivent!*" and went back to sleep.

Students had been selected on the basis of quotas assigned to all units of American troops in E.T.O. They were required to be high school graduates, and in many cases they had to take competitive examinations administered by the I. and E. staff. Ninety per cent were "noncom's" and enlisted men. The other tenth were officers, and I had a lieutenant colonel and an enlisted man sitting next to each other in one of my classes. There were a few Waac's and army nurses in the quotas. In the first of the three eight-week terms at Biarritz American University, there were thirty-nine hundred students enrolled; in the second term we had forty-two hundred; and in the third and last the number fell to twenty-three hundred. In each term we had a new body of students except for the top 2 per cent, who were allowed to stay over if they wished. In general, our students were intelligent, ambitious, and industrious. They were happy to be at B.A.U., appreciative of our efforts, and willing to overlook the shortcomings of our operation.

What were these GI's looking for at our university? Many hoped to accumulate scholastic credits that would be transferable to home colleges, and I believe that such credits were generally accepted and applied on earnings for degrees. Others sought merely a means of occupying their time more profitably and pleasantly than in camp routines; one of the most popular of our "sections" was that of the fine arts, which included music and radio as well as the graphic and plastic arts. Still others hoped to find courses that would be immediately helpful on demobilization, which probably accounts for the fact that the commerce section showed the largest enrollment of any department in the university.

Schools and colleges were called "sections" at B.A.U., and departments were "branches." Deans were "chiefs," and each "branch" had a "head." There were no ranks among professors; all were "instructors."

The journalism section was assigned to the Villa les Courlis, a commodious three-story house once occupied by the Germans as headquarters for the bureau that had supervised agricultural operations in southern France during the occupation. There we established offices, set up classrooms, and installed a newsroom with plenty of typewriters and a copy desk for the daily paper that we hoped to publish both as a laboratory exercise and as a journal of news and information for the whole installation. On my faculty on opening day I had twelve men, and later our number was increased to eighteen. We had over two hundred students the first term.

The *B.A.U. Banner*, with all of its faults, was a minor miracle. At six o'clock every afternoon, Monday through Friday, we took over the plant of the *Journal de Biarritz*, a small afternoon paper, and produced therefrom a morning paper of four tabloid-size pages, which we delivered free to all the messes of the installation in time for breakfast. Print-paper was my greatest headache, but there were other troubles. The press and linotypes of the

Journal were inadequate for that paper alone, and there were numberless mechanical difficulties. I was on the telephone to Paris nearly every day for weeks trying to get GI linotype operators and pressmen. I knew there must be hundreds of them in the American forces in E.T.O., but it was not until the day after the University had begun its first term that one appeared. Then in walked Staff Sergeant Jabonski, a man of many resources and lately a linotype operator in Brooklyn. I felt like kissing him on both cheeks, with Gallic exuberance. A few days later we were sent another operator, and then they kept coming until we had to turn them away. There were two old linotypes long out of commission, and our boys managed to repair them so that they gave us some help. "Mats" were badly "beat up," and replacements were difficult to obtain. Future perusers of the file of the little old *Banner* may wonder at the recurrence of wrong-font *l*'s in the body type of certain early numbers. Blame not the proofreader, O future peruser, for as often as he marked the letter "w.f.," so often it reappeared in its same state; what was there to put in its place?

In the paragraph about the *Banner* in our "yearbook," Churchill was paraphrased: "Never was so much work done by so many to so little avail." What devoted effort on the part of students and faculty went into the pages of that tawdry little sheet! How many mornings did the army's "two hours" find a tired band devouring a late snack of that execrable porridge that B.A.U. messes relied upon to fill empty stomachs and reluctantly provided at early cockcrow for us and the night MP's. We were a tired band indeed, but triumphant, for once more the *B.A.U. Banner* had come out!

I have just been going over my own treasured file of the paper; and I am impressed by the fact that in spite of battered equipment, insufficient mechanical help, lack of proper paper, and the necessity of using printers who knew no English to set heads and make up forms, we put out a newsy, interesting, amusing paper. We carried Associated Press and Army News Service wire reports. We made a great hit by featuring detailed stories the morning after each of the world's series baseball games. We printed Washington news, the latest information from the Japanese occupation, and the reports and rumors about units bound stateside; but a large part of our stuff was local. At first we were criticized for printing too many pictures of near-nudity on the beach, and we toned that down a bit; but we printed Sansone and other favorite cartoonists of the GI's.

Also we issued a yearbook of pictures and summary sketches of the various university operations, called *B.A.U. Beacon.* C. J. ("Mex") Medlin, on leave from Kansas State College, had charge of this project. He had most of his engraving and printing done at Bordeaux, a hundred and fifty miles to the northward; and to correlate the work of our own photographers and editors with that of temperamental French workmen so far away was no small feat. "Mex" was a specialist in college annuals at home, and the *Beacon* was his own baby; but his practical knowledge of printing made him invaluable to the *Banner* as well. He was my roommate at the Miramar and my "buddy" throughout the whole B.A.U. adventure. His sense of humor saved many a situation. His command of the French language was extremely limited, but he could get along with the French printers better than anybody else in our group.

And with the Basques, too. There were many of these interesting people, so different from their French compatriots in many ways, in our neighborhood of Biarritz and Bayonne. One of the best printers in the *Journal-Banner* shop was a Basque named Joseph. He was a tall, well-proportioned man, with a prominent Grecian nose, who was never seen without a beret, indoors or out. "Mex" went fishing with him, overlooked his "make-up" of *Banner* forms, and managed to communicate by grunts, pointing, and a few words they had in common.

One of the most interesting of our journalism courses was the one in "feature writing," conducted by T-4 Murray T. Bloom, who was a successful free-lance writer in private life. He had a class of thirty or forty lively-minded students who, operating through the army's special services, promoted a number of excursions to interesting places in southern France on week ends. Did they not have to dig up picturesque material on which to build their feature stories? And what could be better than the little "republic" of Andorra in the foothills of the Pyrenees? Or a pilgrimage to Lourdes? Or a visit to the world-famous vineyard at Château Yquem? Or a bullfight at Dax? Thus the boys enjoyed some lively and informal tourism, riding in half-trucks and jeeps. And of course I went along on these junkets whenever I could get away.

Other classes in the various sections of our university made varied excursions throughout France. Industrial, agricultural, and engineering operations were studied on the spot; flora, fauna, and geological formations were investigated on field trips. The Vézère valley caves were explored by the anthropologists and artists. Art classes made week-end trips to Paris.

These expeditions were by no means the only extra-curricular activities of Biarritz American University. Always there was the beach. On fair days it was beautiful in the pastel colors and the silver that gave the coast the name Côte d'Argent. Hundreds of our students would lie out on the beach in the late afternoon with their books, acquiring knowledge and a tan at the same time. In bad weather *la grande plage* was off bounds, but the view from the great windows of the hotels and some of the villas was always magnificent. Better yet on stormy days was a walk along the esplanade, where you not only had a view of the greys and blacks and purples and greens of the sea, with the white foam on the crests of the great breakers, but you also received little lashes of that foam in your face, and you had to shoulder into the wind to make your way along the high, narrow walk.

The plays produced by the drama branch of B.A.U. were memorable. Hubert C. Hefner, on leave from Stanford, headed that branch, and he had the services of a number of distinguished men of the theater, such as Guthrie McClintic and Richard Whorf. I remember particularly the uninhibited productions of *The Front Page* and *You Can't Take It with You* in the first term, and the more finished presentations of *Richard III* and *Winterset* in the second term.

There were three terms of eight weeks each at B.A.U., with intervening periods of two weeks. In the vacation time between the first and second terms, I was one of seven men who were scheduled to make lecture tours in central Germany. I spoke at American air service installations from Bad Kissingen south to Munich. My chief memories of that rather difficult assignment are of the towering piles of rubble and the wrecked streets in Nuremberg and other cities, of small and bored audiences, and of interesting rides through Bavaria by plane and automobile. Driving from Bad Kissingen down to Ansbach, we went a few kilometers out of our way to see the famous old walled town of Rothenburg—a relic of Franconian Bavaria, its old houses of stone and colored tiles all like a picture in a child's storybook. At least, that was what my friend Carl Taeusch (Harvard) who as a boy had visited grandparents in Bavaria, told Jim Umstattd (Texas) and me, his traveling companions. But what did we find? When we passed through the arched gate in the old wall, we found what seemed to be complete destruction—all rubble and desolation. We could drive in only a short distance, and had to back out because barriers blocked our way. We were told later that one night toward the end of the war, an American bomber had mistaken its target and had dropped its load on Rothenburg by mistake. I understand that the old town has since been restored and is again a reminder of picturesque ancient Bavaria.

Shrivenham was closed after two terms. B.A.U.'s orders to shut down were countermanded at the last moment, however, and preparations went forward there for a third term, with a decreased enrollment in prospect. The time of greatest need for the university had passed; the larger part of the great stateside transport operation had been accomplished. I turned the administrative responsibilities of the journalism section over to able, brilliant Max Grossman, of Boston University, and retreated in good order to the Zone of the Interior.

We who served on the faculties of the Army universities found our work, though not without its hardships, one of the most stimulating educational experiences of our lives. We felt that the double project at Shrivenham and Biarritz had been a success from nearly all points of view, and we ourselves learned many things from it. It was a good transition for the students from army back to school; but it was a good preparation, too, for the faculty in dealing with the large numbers of veterans who were soon to flood into our colleges and universities under what was called "the GI Bill of Rights."

13

Mission to Japan

"WAR DEPARTMENT EXPERT" was the flattering title that I bore during my visit to occupied Japan in the spring of 1947. It would have been even more flattering if there had not been "experts" to right of me, "experts" to left of me, volleying and thundering.

I went to Japan as consultant to the Press and Publications Department (P.&P.) of the Civil Information and Education Division (C.I.&E.) of the Supreme Command, Allies of the Pacific (SCAP). That is a lot of alphabet, but work and life were adjusted to bureaus with such lettered designations during the occupation years in Japan. Mine was a double task: I was expected to advise Japanese newspaper management about the ethics and business of journalism under a democratic ideology and to counsel Japanese university authorities in regard to education for journalism. All the time I was there, I found myself hoping that my Japanese friends were not as conscious of the limitations of my knowledge as I was.

I went to Washington for briefing and then flew nearly ten thousand miles to Tokyo. Much of this plane travel was fairly comfortable. We had what they called "a plush job"—the C-54 "Statesman," which carried proper seats for passengers—from Washington to San Francisco; but our planes over the Pacific were fitted with what were known as "bucket seats," on which I shall not particularize further than to say that they were apparently designed for discomfort on long trips.

We were laid over a day in San Francisco waiting for a plane, and I took the opportunity to pay a visit to Paul C. Smith, then editor of the *Chronicle,* who took me out to his house for lunch. Paul's house hung to the precipitous side of Telegraph Hill, and from his glassed-in dining room he had the finest view of its kind I ever saw from any home—the whole of San Francisco Bay, the perfection of the Golden Gate Bridge, the cities on the other side plainly seen, the ocean blue and alluring beyond and beyond. The other guest at that luncheon was Thorsten Brandel, the Swedish consul to San Francisco, an interesting and cultivated person. Over our manhattans, I told my fellow guest I was on my way to Tokyo; and he then remarked that he had just put a Ford aboard ship for his colleague in that city. I note this circumstance because less than a week later, in Tokyo, my friend Charles E. Tuttle (whom I had known in the States in connection with his family's rare book business at Rutland, Vermont) took me out to visit his quarters and stopped somewhere amid the maze of streets to make a call on a friend whom he introduced as "Harry," with a last name that I did not catch.

"I was just mixing a drink," said Harry. "What will you have?"

The manhattans we were soon sipping reminded me of that view from Paul Smith's windows and of that pleasant person, the Swedish consul. But as soon as I mentioned Mr. Brandel's name, Harry burst out with expletives.

"That rascal! That scamp!" he exclaimed. "That

bluffer! He has been promising to send me an automobile for three years, and it isn't here yet!"

I then realized that Harry was no other than the Swedish consul to Tokyo, and I was able to say to him, "Calm yourself, Harry. Your automobile is on the way. Your San Francisco colleague has not only placed it aboard ship, but he has sent me on ahead to announce to you that it is coming!"

One of the pleasures of social intercourse is the exploitation of mutual acquaintanceships, and that game is even more exciting when played abroad. On the little promenade at the airstrip at Guam, when our plane put down there one midnight, I fell into conversation with a colonel stationed on that island, to find that we knew and liked some of the same people in Burlington, Vermont. Colonel John A. Jimerson, a Nebraskan who had befriended me in Paris and Biarritz, appeared again in Tokyo to renew his favors. And former students! I have long had the delightful experience of finding them wherever I have gone.

Flying the Pacific was an adventure which held many compensations for the "bucket seats" and the overcrowding of the ship. The stops at Honolulu, Johnston Island, Kwajalein, Guam, and Iwo Jima were full of interest. I remember well a few unbelievably beautiful glimpses of coral isles and shoals in pastel tints far below us somewhere east of the China Sea. There were many interesting persons aboard. Frederick G. Melcher, editor of *Publishers' Weekly,* going over as an expert on book publishing and libraries, was a pleasant traveling companion. We were in the air almost forty hours between San Francisco and Tokyo.

I had the good fortune to visit Japan in the second half of the second year of the occupation, when most of the SCAP reforms had been put into operation and were showing results. It was a major social and economic revolution that Japan was undergoing. Chief architect of the new system was General Douglas MacArthur, who had the benefit of counsel from many well-informed students of Japanese history, economics, and society. Many of the reforms had been effected by military decree, and a threatened general strike had been prevented by show of military force; but at the time of my visit, most of the changes were being made by laws passed by a freely elected Diet.

Fundamental in the revolution was the fall of Tenno, the god-emperor ideology. I think that higher classes of Japanese witnessed this phenomenon with something more than equanimity. Shinto in general, however, as far as my information extends, did not suffer attack from the new regime. I became much interested in this national religion of Japan and had some long conversations with the priest who had charge of the great Shinto shrine above Yokohama harbor. He and his wife were charming, sensitive, and informed persons. From talks with them and with others, I received the impression that Shinto today is somewhat less a body of principles that its adherents live by and would die for than it is a great treasury of aesthetic achievement and vision.

More important in the democratization of Japan than the collapse of Tenno was the annihilation of the monopolistic system which had grown to amazing proportions before the war, when Mitsui and Mitsubishi became national super-monopolies, and which was now broken up.

Land reform was also basic in the MacArthur revolution. The Second Land Reform Act was passed by the Diet a few months before my visit, and I had the opportunity of seeing it at work. It provided that large

holdings of tenant-farmed lands owned by absentee land-
lords should be subject to compulsory sale on reasonable
terms. Thus at last the farmers themselves received a
chance to own the land they tilled.

I found these "little farmers" an interesting feature
of the Japanese scene. All over Japan I saw them—men,
women, and children—toiling in their rice paddies or
garden plots. They were doing everything by hand, with
the most primitive farming implements. They drilled
in wheat in rows by hand, and it looked luxuriant—already
heading out in central Honshu in late April of 1947.
Rarely do these families use animals for farm operations,
though cows and oxen are used for hauling. On Hokkaido, the big northern island, I saw more horses and
more animals in the field than on Honshu or Kyushu; up
there, too, they were doing more dairying.

Individual farms rarely exceed three acres; usually
they are smaller than that. The soil is rich, where it is
arable at all. It is continually enriched by fertilizers,
notably by human excrement. This "night soil," as it is
modestly called, may once have been transported by
night; but today the carts carrying it are a familiar day-
time sight on all Japanese highways. I was told that
only sixteen per cent of the area of Japan is arable, however. On one of my assignments, I had to fly over Honshu
from Tokyo to the northeastern tip of the island; and I
then looked down on an unbroken succession of volcanic
ridges and peaks, with roads and green plots only in the
deep and narrow valleys. In some districts, mountain-
sides were terraced for farming, but the proportion of
Japan's mountains so used is small.

Another interesting phase of democratic reform in
Japan was the change in the status of women. Whatever
may be said in defense of the old Japanese family system,

there can be no doubt that in general it did not give women a fair chance. But under the occupation they gained the right to vote, and when I was there they had more than fifty seats in the Diet. And perhaps more importantly, they were attaining something like equality in the educational system. My discussions with several prominent women—on education, economics, politics, and social reform—stand out in my memory.

My chief work in Japan was, as I have said, with the Civil Information and Education Division of SCAP. I found that agency composed of well-informed, well-balanced, hard-working, devoted men and women who were co-operating with Japanese schools, press, and other social agencies to devise and put into effect the most workable means of teaching democracy to the people. I felt that they were engaged in a highly unified effort and that they knew what they were doing. I know that some American critics of the effort did not agree with this evaluation. One great newspaper, speaking editorially of our campaign, called "democracy" a tired word. I do confess that my own preaching about our creed involved much soul searching. We all had to admit, under the probing, never-ending questioning of our Japanese friends, that in America we fall short of the mark of our high calling in many respects and on many fronts. But for us and for the people we were trying to help, "democracy" was a very lively word—indeed, almost a magic word. Certainly it was the watchword of the MacArthur revolution in Japan.

In writing of the C.I.&E. Division of SCAP, I do not wish to underrate the work of the I.&E. staffs of the military government. By rugged jeep and by wearisome and uncomfortable train, these army men carried the teaching of democracy even to remote provincial villages.

They checked on a new school system which was no longer regimented from Tokyo, which had thrown out the old military-feudalistic textbooks in favor of some that were in step with the modern world, which now admitted girls on an equal basis with boys, and which had extended compulsory school attendance from six to nine years.

My own educational work was specialized and limited. I visited a dozen of Japan's chief institutions of higher education, conferring with executives about the possibility of establishing schools of journalism; and I held regular conferences for representatives of Tokyo universities to the same end. I learned that the first journalism education in Japan had been undertaken under the inspiration of a visit by my famous predecessor in the deanship of the Missouri School of Journalism, Walter Williams, in 1925, when Hideo Ono, then a sub-editor of *Nichi-Nichi*, had begun a series of lectures on the history of the Japanese press at Tokyo Imperial University. Eventually, however, the pattern in Japan had come to follow the German concept of education in this field—partly because of Professor Ono's sojourn in Zurich and partly because the German plan called for no laboratory equipment or even any close relations with the working press. In all of my conferences with educators in Japan, I advocated the American tripartite pattern of education for journalism, which (1) assures sound and full liberal arts backgrounds, (2) provides adequate laboratory training in techniques and skills, and (3) supplies authoritative guidance in research studies of the press and its relations.

I may have done some good in this advocacy. In the decade since my mission to Japan, I have heard occasional reports and generous comments that help me to believe what I should prefer to believe about my efforts in

this direction.   But education for journalism in Japan
faces conditions different from those in America.   In the
first place, the newspapers are greatly over-staffed, so
that they take on only a few new men each year.   And
then, the great papers have elaborate apprentice courses
which entail lectures, roundtables, guided activities, and
internships for those they do take on.   For such work
they can easily spare teachers from their own staffs.   On
the *Mainichi,* which has perhaps the most extensive course
of this kind, the apprenticeship lasts a year and a half.
Studies appraising the efficacy of this system are lacking,
but it seems to satisfy management on some papers—at
least in default of all-round courses in the schools.

My work directly with the press was highly stimulating
to me.   These activities were within the Press and Publications Department of C.I.&E., which was directed by
Major (later Lieutenant Colonel) Daniel C. Imboden,
a man of rugged Lincolnian type, a true crusader and
zealot.   Imboden was doing his level best to reconcile
wartime controls with available freedom of the press, all
for the good of democracy and SCAP and General Mac-
Arthur.   The unions did not like the major very well
because he had swung SCAP against them when they had
made their big bid to take over total management of the
newspapers in 1946.   The managers did not like him very
well because he stood out against their attempts to raise
subscription rates.   But they all respected his uncom-
promising honesty and his devotion to the welfare of the
press within the ring of SCAP administration.

The Japanese are avid newspaper readers.   Going to
my office every morning at eight, I always saw two
ragged shoemakers with their kits and materials all laid
out on the pavement at an alley corner, but both with
their faces buried in newspapers and oblivious to passers-

by. Every morning they put first things first, as the American businessman does at breakfast, and started the day with the latest news. Hungry, perhaps, and even homeless since the bombing, but never newspaperless. Though distribution of papers is mainly by carrier, casual buyers will actually queue up in the late afternoon in lines of fifty to a hundred to get their papers from curb-side dealers. In many a poor man's budget, newspapers have a priority over rice and fish. When I was in Japan, three Tokyo dailies and two in Osaka each had over a million circulation. Now, fourteen years later, Japan has a circulation of fourteen million daily papers—far more than any other country in the world. (That other island empire, Britain, comes next, with eight.)

During my stay in Japan, I had conferences with groups representing the operation of nearly all of the great newspapers of that country. The activities of a Japanese paper—editorial, business, or mechanical—are subdivided and assigned severally to worker groups known as "sections," and on my visit to the *Tokyo Asahi*, for example, I met some twenty-five heads of "sections" around a big table in their board room. We tossed questions and answers back and forth for an hour and a quarter, and then I suggested that they had probably had enough; but they kept it up for an hour longer.

These Japanese newspapermen were thoughtful and sharp-minded. They were eager to know about customs, practices, ideas, and plans related to all phases of the newspaper business and profession—especially in the United States, but also in England and France, which I had visited recently. I was not in uniform, and I was anxious that there should be no barriers of resentment or protocol to interfere with ease of communication. Always there were some refreshments on the table—confections, fruit, tea, and sometimes liquor. I took along no interpreter to these conferences, for I always found someone in the group who knew English well enough to translate for the others—often a man who had served as an American or English correspondent. When I could not answer a question, I said so, and we passed to something else. When my answer was mere opinion, I was careful to label it so, in order not to embarrass P.&P. or the great background power of SCAP. I asked many questions myself; thus I learned much and also greased the wheels of our conferences.

I inspected many great printing plants. A few of them had been injured by bombing, as that of the *Tokyo Shimbun.* Japanese cities, composed mainly of low wooden buildings, suffered their war damage chiefly from incendiary, not demolition, bombs; thus, instead of hills or rubble, as in Germany, one saw in Japan miles of burned-over districts. There was, however, some demolition bombing in Tokyo; unfortunately one university— Keio—was hard hit. I looked into what had been the entrance lobby of the Keio library building through a gap in the wall and saw headless statues and crumbled arches. One of the latter had borne an inscription.

"What does it say?" I asked my professor-guide.

"It is a Japanese version of your western proverb, 'The pen is mightier than the sword,'" he answered, and smiled.

But to continue about Japanese printing plants. I never ceased to marvel at their typesetting operation. There are said to be some nine thousand different ideographs used in Japanese printing; and for such serious prose as is found in newspaper editorials, at least half that number must be available. When I was there, a movement was on foot to reduce the number of characters used in the newspapers; at the *Asahi* they had set a maximum of eighteen hundred. But even if the number of characters used is actually brought down to such a figure, a typesetter has to do a lot of footwork, scampering down the aisles between the high cases of type with his copy tucked in under the composing stick in his left hand, picking up the necessary type for even a short article. After it is used, the type is not distributed, but melted up; and the cases are continually replenished from casting machines. Plants are generally well equipped with excellent perfecting presses, typecasters, teletype communication, and extensive photographic and engraving devices.

With few exceptions, I found Japanese newspapermen affable, courteous, and hospitable. Indeed, before I finished my visit, I was so embarrassed by a plethora of offers of dinners to "Doctor Motto" (as I was often called) that I had to turn such matters over to a man in Major Imboden's department who was an adept in making a "No, thank you" sound like a compliment.

Instructions to all military and civilian personnel in Japan were strict in forbidding eating in the teahouses— not because of the "fraternizing" involved, but because food quotas were on a low level, and any Japanese who entertained guests had to send into the black market for his supplies. My intentions in this matter were good, especially at the beginning of my visit. My very first newspaper call in Japan was made on the *Tokyo Shimbun,* which had that priority on the list made up for me because its managing editor, Kyosuke Fukada, had many years earlier been a student at the Missouri School of Journalism. I found the Fukadas, father and son, pleasant and highly intelligent men. During my morning's conference with the *Shimbun's* section heads, we had some light refreshments—confections, oranges, tea—and when the elder Mr. Fukada said they were giving me lunch, I supposed that was it. After the conference, I was led to a waiting sedan, which was soon filled by the driver, the two Fukadas, their managing director, and Doctor Motto. I thought it was rather an excess of politeness for them all to accompany me on my return to my hotel, but I was unfamiliar with Japanese customs and decided this was merely another example of their famed courtesy. However, I soon realized that we were not setting off toward the hotel at all.

"Where are we going now?" I asked.

"To a small teahouse for lunch," replied the elder Mr. Fukada.

"I'm very sorry," I said, "but I'm afraid I can't go to a teahouse with you. Our rules seem quite definite about that."

"I think General MacArthur would make an exception of this case," argued Mr. Fukada.

"But he hasn't," I countered. "I spent an hour last night reading his instructions on these matters. They are very clear."

"Americans are sometimes entertained in our homes," observed Mr. Fukada.

"Well," I said, "I'm not so sure about that——"

"Then it is all right," declared Mr. Fukada happily. "This small teahouse is just like home. My father was well acquainted with the father of the woman who runs it. It is very small, very nice, just like home."

"I have my doubts——" I protested.

"Here we are," Mr. Fukada said, as our car stopped in front of a rather imposing place. "Just like home," he beamed.

So we had lunch at the teahouse, and a good and interesting meal it was—bits of raw fish and shrimps, each with its separate sauce; sukiyaki in full style and very fine; watergrown potatoes, watercress, noodles, confections, and tea and saki throughout. It was three o'clock before I got back to my office.

A week or two later, a member of the Diet from Kyushu, a Missouri journalism alumnus, gave me a small dinner at a pleasant teahouse in Tokyo. As the sukiyaki was being prepared at the table, the proprietor entered our room noiselessly by the sliding door and whispered to our host, apparently in some alarm. Low-toned Japanese conversation ensued; then the proprietor smiled and bowed and withdrew.

"I'm curious," I remarked, "to know what's going on."

"He says," explained my host, with a nod toward the door, "that the military police have driven off an American car from in front of the teahouse. He was afraid it belonged to our party. I told him we all came on foot. So that is all right." And my host smiled widely under his mustache.

I was glad I had insisted on walking the short distance from my hotel, but not even the good food and plentiful saki could prevent my worrying about my shoes. Of course, we had left our shoes at the entrance to the teahouse; and if the MP's would drive off an American car, might they not also carry off American shoes? I foresaw myself walking home over cobbled streets in my socks. Not until the party was over was I completely reassured; then the servants brought out our shoes, which they had sequestered in a safe place, helped us put them on, and afterward stood in a row on the teahouse porch in the moonlight, bowing and smiling goodnight in that lovely way the Japanese have of speeding the parting guest.

The most beautiful teahouse at which I was entertained during my "tour of duty" in Japan was the famous

House of the Crane, in the edge of Kyoto. It is distinguished by the simplicity in which the Japanese excel
—a few fine paintings, a few richly beautiful hangings,
a single fine flower arrangement in a niche. The rooms
face inward upon a formal garden that displays rock,
water, trees, and flower effects, and includes a miniature
shrine and a summer house. At the luncheon, my hosts,
the editors of the *Kyoto Shimbun,* had provided a geisha
dance as a special attraction. The geisha girls paint their
faces white, place flowers in their elaborate coiffures,
and wear obis that flow down the back instead of being
folded in big formal bows. Their kimonos are so long
that they lie out on the floor several inches around them,
and walking in them is an art. The dances are stylized
and highly symbolic.

It was also in Kyoto that I attended a garden party
given by a newly elected mayor, at which there was a
series of symbolic dances—some of them grotesque *bu-
gaku* by men with masks and magnificent costumes, some
of them charming mimes by geisha. Finally the geisha
danced and sang the famous "Four Seasons of Kyoto"—
including the cherry-blossom season, when, as our program put it, "all the people are on the spree, with the
heart softened."

They were really on the spree at Arashiyama Park the
last night of the cherry-blossom festival in Kyoto.

"Have you learned to distinguish the Koreans from the
Japanese?" asked my guide from the *Shimbun.*

"I'm afraid not," I confessed.

"It is easy: the intoxicated ones are the Koreans,"
said my guide without a smile. I think he was pulling
my leg—or else Korea had sent an exceptionally large
delegation to this festival.

The petals of the cherry blossoms were falling when I

was in Kyoto. Shall I ever forget a glimpse of a lagoon with its surface covered with fallen pink petals? Or standing under a special tree whose down-swept branches closed me into a cell of rosy bloom? There are said to be some thirty-five species of flowering cherries, some blooming earlier and some later, so that the season dies slowly with lingering beauty.

Another interesting assignment called for a trip to Hokkaido, Japan's northern island. At Ito, not much over fifty miles southwest of Tokyo, I had picked oranges from the trees one week end; and the next I was in a land that was just emerging from deep winter cold. I was greatly impressed with what I thought of as Japan's Alaska, with the broad scale of its scene in comparison with that of Honshu and with the enterprise of its capital, Sapporo.

In connection with my chief address at Sapporo, I was the victim of the worst interpreter's "snafu" in my experience. Or rather, my audience was the victim of this misadventure. The young Japanese assigned to be my interpreter was a bright, self-confident instructor in the city's university. I should have been more cautious about lending him my manuscript notes in advance. What he did when he had them in hand was to translate the whole thing into written Japanese—a task which I think he must have sat up all night to perform. But when I gave the address, I spoke a few sentences as usual and then waited for the interpreter to interpret. What he did was to read off what he took to be the corresponding piece of his Japanese manuscript. We had not continued this game for long before we were miles apart, and when I ad-libbed or skipped, my partner was in a maze. Finally I realized that I was merely shadowboxing, and said to the young interpreter, "Go on, read 'em what you've got!" and sat down. It did not take long to wind up the affair.

The audience did not laugh, and it applauded courteously at the end, but I think that it was more than a little mystified by the whole proceeding.

In speaking to an audience in a language that it did not understand, I always hoped to make my gestures and emphasis carry some of the platform emotion through the interpreter-medium to the hearers. It was disconcerting, nevertheless, to realize that I was always being edited, consciously or not, in translation. I was usually curious, too, about what the man who introduced me was saying. When I made my major address in Tokyo, I was introduced by Seitoku Ito, publisher of *Jiji Simpo*—a fine gentleman who was at the time president of the Japan Newspaper Editors' and Publishers' Association. I was sitting off the platform, at one side, with that best of interpreters, Mr. Ohno, of P.&P. The introduction was interrupted by a spontaneous burst of applause, during which many faces were turned in my direction, all smiling and nodding. I whispered to Mr. Ohno, "What in the world is he saying?" "He is telling them," my interpreter smiled, "that this is your birthday." Sure enough, it was, and Mr. Ito had dug up that little fact when he had "researched" my life and works for the purpose of his introduction.

But we must return to Hokkaido, if only to get out of it. While I was still at Sapporo, the seasonal thaw had set in. Late spring had come on fast; the ground, which had been hard with frost, was suddenly soft and muddy, and, as they say, the "bottom" had gone out of the roads. I was ready now to fly back to Tokyo, but the airport nearest Sapporo is at Chitose, thirty miles away.

"The road to Chitose is absolutely impassable," said the commandant, a very decided man who headed a very brass-bound installation. "You'll have to go by rail."

"But that will take a day's travel on a very poor train," I complained. I had heard about that trip.

"That's the way it is," snapped the commandant. I could see him thinking: *These civilians!*

"But listen, Colonel," I said. "You give me a jeep and a GI driver, and I promise you we'll get through. And I'm willing to wager I'll catch my plane and be in Tokyo tomorrow night." I had known mudholes in Iowa, and I was sure Hokkaido had no worse ones. Besides, I had great faith in jeeps and GI drivers.

"You're a stubborn fellow," said the Colonel as he signed the order. "I don't think you'll get through."

We left at seven o'clock the next morning, and in the next few hours we negotiated some of the worst road I ever saw, filled with chuck-holes and occasional sloughs of mud that seemed to have no bottoms. Once I thought we were stuck for good, half buried in mud. That time, instead of reaching for the shovels, my driver seized his camera, cried "I'm a picture-bug!" and leaped out of the car. I later saw the shots he got of that scene, and they were pretty good, showing about two-thirds of the car above the circumambient mud. I think we should not have been able to work ourselves out of that one, and I should have lost my bet with the Colonel, except for the help of three or four Japanese farmers. I believe they may have been Ainus, from their stature and hairy faces. At any rate, they appeared providentially from nowhere, bringing fence-rails, and got us out of one mudhole and into another, and then out of that one. There were twenty minutes to spare before plane time when we reached Chitose, but it took me a long time to get over the bruises and exertions of that morning.

As I look back upon the many interviews I had while

on my mission to Japan, a few personalities stand out in my memory.

Tsunega Baba, director of *Yomiuri,* one of the leading Japanese newspapers, was a striking individual. He was taller than most Japanese, lantern-jawed, and displayed a firm mouth and chin. The left side of his face was scarred, the result of I do not know which of the conflicts of a tumultuous career. He seemed to me a scholar and a gentleman, gifted with the ability to express smoothly ideas that embodied much common sense. He, more than any other Japanese, had been responsible for the defeat of an early communist plan for the unions to take over the whole editorial, business, and mechanical management of the country's newspapers. The first drive of this campaign had been made on the *Yomiuri;* and it was Baba's firm stand, judiciously supported by P.&P., that had defeated the grand project.

Of all the women I met in Japan, Motoko Hani was the most remarkable. A short, stocky woman, she made a deceptively undistinguished appearance. When I interviewed her, her eyes were almost closed against the light and her face was not expressive; but her talk was keen-minded, original, and bold. Founder of *Fujin no Tomo,* the first women's magazine in Japan, she and her husband had used its profits to start a notably liberal coeducational school on the edge of Tokyo, Jiyu Gakuen (Freedom School). Frank Lloyd Wright had designed its buildings. When the American educational commission came to Japan in 1946, some of its members visited Jiyu Gakuen and reported that Japanese educators need not look to foreign schools to observe some of the most advanced modern practices in successful operation but could find them right there in the Hani school. My own

visit to this institution was one of the highlights of my
Japanese sojourn.

I found Shigeru Nambara, president of Tokyo University (it had recently dropped the word "Imperial"
from its name), a man of rare and sensitive intelligence.
A handsome grey man, with a thinker's eyes and countenance, he spoke easily and convincingly. I spent most
of one afternoon in conversation with him in his office at
the University. I have often recalled the conviction with
which he argued then to the effect that the Japanese
people were welcoming the democratic philosophy which
we were bringing them because, after all, individual
rights are fundamental in the minds of all human beings.
All through the feudal and militaristic regimes in Japan,
he said, a certain core of human-rights belief had remained in the people, whatever their leaders had said
and done. Now that Japan was living in a climate of
ideas friendly to individualism and getting some start
with democratic processes, he reasoned, it was unlikely
ever to be willing to abandon this freer exercise of opinion
and action. I am sure Doctor Nambara believed this; and
I certainly wanted to, for it was the basis for most of the
civilian effort in the occupation.

I did not meet General MacArthur until ten days
before my departure from Japan. I then sent "through
channels" a request for an appointment chiefly because
I wished to pay the head of the organization for which I
had been working a short courtesy call.

The General's popularity ran very high in Tokyo at
that time. In the States I had heard some returned
GI's say abusive things about him, but I found that the
Armed Forces in Japan when I was there idolized him.
The civilians who worked under SCAP also generally
thought highly of him, while the Japanese people often

seemed to go further than any others in the MacArthur craze. Every day when he left the Dai-ichi Building, in which he had his offices, to go out for lunch, there were literally hundreds of curious persons crowded about the entrance to catch a sight of him, many of them with cameras in hand. I was told that the General had appointed one of his staff to count and report the exact size of this "gallery" each day, but that may be a slander. On the day I visited Dai-ichi, I heard there had been almost a thousand people at the luncheon appearance—a record count.

My interview with General MacArthur surprised me in several ways. I had expected to find a man who would typify "top brass," dignified and curt, and give me my few minutes only as an official duty. But the General without the military hat in which he was so often photographed, a big black pipe in his mouth and his leg cocked up over the arm of an overstuffed chair, was a new MacArthur to me. He seemed to have a rather benevolent look and a kinder, if older, countenance than his pictures showed. He proved to be a remarkable conversationalist, talking easily, with a rapid flow of ideas. I was amazed when, after a while, I glanced at my watch: I had been there an hour! I rose apologetically to go, but the General waved me down; he had some more things to discuss. So I remained nearly half an hour longer.

MacArthur was then much concerned about the tardiness of the Allied Powers in making a peace treaty with Japan and thus allowing the nation to work out an economic plan that would ward off starvation for a considerable proportion of its people.

"If that is not done soon," he declared, "I will not be responsible for what may happen."

"What do you mean by soon?" I asked.

"Just as soon as Marshall gets back from the debacle he is making in Europe, he should get busy on the peace treaty," said the General with feeling.

He could see local insurrections if something along this line were not done soon, but he was not afraid of either a return to militarism on the part of the "Nips," as he called them, or a turn to communism after the peace and the end of the occupation.

"But," I said, "won't the Reds slip in when we march out? Just last week I saw a Soviet parade in downtown Tokyo in which scores, maybe hundreds, of Japanese marched with the red flag flying in front."

"Oh, anybody will follow a band," the General said. "I hope you noticed what a setback the Reds got in the election last month?"

Indeed I had. They had won only a few seats in the Diet. General MacArthur agreed with President Nambara in the view he had expressed to me some weeks earlier, that the Japanese had never been completely committed to militarism but that their docility had betrayed them. The General was sure that the stage was now set for a self-maintaining economy, provided the fetters of military occupation and the threat of crippling reparations were removed, so that an international trade system could be established. We talked also of newspapers, of universities, of the Nipponese character. I was flattered to find that the General had got himself briefed on my own activities and speeches; and I was tremendously impressed by the breadth and variety of his detailed information, not only on occupation activities but on affairs in the States.

The fact is, I was virtually hypnotized by the MacArthur personality. I enjoyed that hour-and-a-half visit hugely. When I finally broke away, the General followed me into the outer office, gave me over to the charge of an aide to return me to my quarters, shook hands with me, and finally put his hand on my shoulder and said, "Mr. Mott, I realize that you have come over to help us at much personal sacrifice, and I want you to know that your country appreciates it!" Well, I walked out of that room simply treading on air, and it was at least an hour before I emerged partially from the spell I had been under.

I have never met a more magnetic character than General MacArthur. A few years later General Ginsburg told me that Raymond Clapper, the famous newspaper correspondent had once related to him an experience similar to mine. After an interview with MacArthur, Clapper had walked the Tokyo streets for an hour trying to shake off the spell. "I will not send my story," he declared, "until I am free of that fantastic MacArthur magnetism."

My audience with the Emperor Hirohito came about through a chain of circumstances, mainly fortuitous. Shortly after notice of my arrival in Tokyo appeared in the papers, I received an invitation through military channels to have a teahouse luncheon with Tsuneo Matsudaira, former ambassador to the United States. In 1926 Ambassador Matsudaira had visited the University of Missouri in order to present to the School of Journalism, in a gesture of international goodwill, a stone lantern that had formerly stood in the grounds once occupied by the first American legation to Tokyo as a gift from the America-Japan Society of that city. Mr. Matsudaira, now an industrialist in political retirement but a member of the Imperial Household, remembered his visit to the University of Missouri with much pleasure and wished to extend all possible courtesies to a representative of that institution sojourning in Japan. Indeed, he seemed so sincere and emphatic in that wish that it occurred to my friend Colonel Waldon Winston, who had accompanied me to the luncheon, that an audience with the Emperor might be arranged for us through Mr. Matsudaira's interest.

I know very little about the negotiations for that interview, which I understand were extensive and involved various conferences and much paper work. Colonel Winston, who was chief liaison officer between the army and the Japanese government, was adept in such matters; and we were both disappointed when in the final arrangements he was not permitted to accompany me to the palace. Apparently his uniform was unwelcome. I was not as conscious of the importance of uniforms as I should have been, I dare say, since I realized too late that I was probably expected to appear at the palace in diplomatic garb—cutaway coat, striped trousers, stand-up collar. At breakfast on the morning of my appointment with the Emperor, friends told me of a delegation of American clergymen who had been granted an imperial audience some weeks earlier and who had all fitted themselves out in the "uniform" I have described. But there I was, in a rather seedy suit of professorial cut—or something of the kind. At any rate, there I was.

It was my luck that morning to draw an ailing car from the C.I.&E. automotive pool, and it balked repeatedly in traffic and only after prolonged agony delivered me inside the grounds. There I was taken in charge by a Japanese guard and conducted to the palace and finally to a broad red-carpeted staircase that I ascended alone. At its top I was met by the imperial chamberlain and Count Matsudaira (no relative of the former ambassador) and three or four other gentlemen, one of whom was later to act as interpreter—all wearing cutaway coats, et cetera. I found the Count an especially affable gentleman. After we had chatted for a few minutes, the Count, glancing at his watch, asked me to accompany him to the audience chamber. We were followed by the interpreter. The room was fairly large and contained a few western-style chairs and a beautiful large gold screen. The interpreter indicated my chair; and I stood beside it as the Emperor, accompanied by two other gentlemen, entered. They were also attired in formal morning apparel.

I do not mean to make too much of this matter of clothes. It did not worry me at the time. I think it was not until I came to write up the episode in my journal somewhat later that I realized there was a sartorial joke on the Missouri professor somewhere in the picture.

The Emperor was a slight figure, with close-clipped mustache and thick-lensed glasses. He greeted me pleasantly, shaking hands with the arm held rather high; then he nodded toward my chair and we both sat, while the others stood, the interpreter by my side. Most of our conversation was formal, beginning with compliments and running on to the kind of inquiry that one commonly makes of a foreign visitor. I was pleased to have the Emperor ask me what my impressions of Japan were, because at this time, just before my departure, I had been summarizing them for myself. I said that my chief impression was gratification over the apparently sincere effort that the people were making to instrument a democratic ideology in all phases of Japanese life. It may be that this was not a sentiment well adapted to the ears of the late incarnation of Tenno, but it was received equably. I added that there were two other things—

very charming elements in the life of Japan that I should always remember: one was the children, those round-faced, bright-eyed little boys and girls that one saw everywhere, well behaved, lively, attractive; and the other was the Japanese gardens, so well cared for and virtually parts of the houses to which they belonged.

The Emperor spoke somewhat hesitantly and entirely in Japanese, of which I knew scarcely a word; but I had the feeling that he understood much of what I had said before the interpreter made his translation. For example, he smiled a little when I spoke of the children. But during most of the interview he did not seem to look directly at me. Perhaps this effect was due to his heavy glasses; perhaps it came from some small nervous mannerisms.

When I led the conversation to political matters, the Emperor observed that Japan was most anxious to re-establish commerce with foreign countries, and he hoped the American press and people would urge our government to make this possible. In my reply, I mentioned the remarks that General MacArthur had made to me on the same subject a week before. Hirohito then observed that Japan owed much to General MacArthur.

A little later the conversation lagged. I realized that it was not my business to end the audience, but I did take occasion to thank the Emperor for his kindness in receiving me. At that point he rose, and of course I did. He shook hands again and said he hoped I would some day return to Japan for a longer visit. He then walked to the door, accompanied by his two attendants; and just before he left the room, he turned and bowed.

After leaving the palace, I was shown, by the Emperor's order, parts of the imperial establishment in which I expressed special interest—the art gallery, the theater, the potting sheds where the dwarf trees were trained, the stables. My moribund C.I.&E. car finally refused to move further, and I had to be taken back to my hotel in a sedan from the imperial household's garage.

Two days later, out in the skies over the Pacific Ocean, somewhere north of Guam, I wrote down in my journal an account of my meeting with the Emperor. I added the following note: "There is a wicked saying in Tokyo that the Trinity is composed of MacArthur, Hirohito, and God. I may have the order wrong, but not the list. I have now had interviews with two of them."

Not half an hour after thus recording a current sacrilege, I heard the shrill peal of the pilot's bell that signified the plane was about to "ditch." We all jumped for our Mae Wests and parachute harnesses—just as we had been instructed repeatedly to do in such an emergency. The traffic clerk leaped into the middle of the deck and shouted: "Take it easy! It's a dry run! I ought to of warned you we were due for this! Get your 'chutes on, but don't get excited!" By the time he was through warning us against panic, we were all equipped for ditching; then, having performed the exercise satisfactorily, we received the pilot's signal, "As you were." As we all agreed later, we had not had time to be frightened; but I remember yet that the thought that flashed through my mind as soon as I heard the peal of that bell was: "Frank Mott, here's your third interview coming up!"

I had always had the fatalistic conviction that if I should ever be on a plane that had to ditch it would be "thirty" for one unseaworthy teacher. But my third interview was postponed, and, aside from the usual delays when changing planes, the return trip to Washington was not unpleasant.

The question that lingered in my mind after the return

from my mission to Japan was, "Is it possible to alter to any considerable degree and with any permanence the ideology of a whole people?" I am still skeptical about it. But if President Nambara was right, perhaps we were helping to guide more than we were altering; and if the nation's leaders are wise, Japan may continue for a long time gaining strength in the set of principles that we call "democracy."

In my interview with General MacArthur, I quoted to him an epigram of Major Imboden's: "The Japanese revolution in democracy is the greatest miracle since the resurrection of Christ." The General smiled. "That is probably an overstatement," he said.

14

A Journalist's Testament

IT WAS IN THE FALL OF 1929 that William Allen White
visited us in Iowa City, holding conferences with students, speaking to classes in journalism, and addressing a
group of newspapermen. Dynamic, genial, full of ideas,
Will White was a welcome guest. The Chamber of
Commerce gave a luncheon for him and the other editors
who were in town, at which the Mayor made the speech
introducing White. Now the Mayor rather fancied himself an orator, and he fairly outdid himself on this occasion. His theme was "The Power of the Press," and
he climbed the lofty peaks of eloquence and soared into
the blue empyrean in his eulogy of the editor, his apostro-
phe to the printing press, and his tribute to the mighty
influence of the newspaper. In the course of time, this
grew a little tiresome; but when, at the close of his
peroration, the Mayor triumphantly presented William
Allen White as the epitome of all this beneficent journalism, Will stood up, his ruddy round face beaming, and
said, "Oh, Mr. Mayor, go on and on and on! I love it!
We all love it!"

The Mayor's address was in line with an old tradition
for such gatherings. It used to be the general custom at
the "editorial conventions" held fifty or sixty years ago
to have on the program at least one oration on "The

Power of the Press," in which highly laudatory things were said, to the great satisfaction of the assembled newspapermen. Those days are gone forever. I have not heard one of those old-fashioned orations for years. Nowadays more realistic attitudes prevail, and newspaper gatherings bring forth discussions of the problems and shortcomings of the press rather than unlimited glorification of its mission and its power.

As far as this "power of the press" and its supposed function of "molding public opinion" is concerned, the honest and dispassionate thinker has to discriminate and to choose his terms with care. A number of years ago I did a study of newspaper support of Presidential candidates for the *Public Opinion Quarterly* which showed that half of our Presidents had been elected in spite of a majority press opposition. This happened even in the era of the highly partisan press; today, when papers generally give their readers in their news columns the leading statements and speeches on both sides and even (in many cases) signed opinion columns on both sides, the fact that a majority of them tag themselves Republican or Democratic and occasionally print partisan editorials of their own is a matter of comparatively small importance.

I have pondered much in connection with both my historical studies and my observation of contemporary journalism upon this matter of "editorial influence" on public opinion. Horace Greeley was believed, by his contemporaries and by later historians, to have exerted a great "influence" on the thinking of his readers. Emerson once wrote that Greeley did "all their thinking and theory" for midwestern farmers "at two dollars a year"— the price of the *Weekly Tribune*. Contemporary Democratic politicians have viewed with alarm the spectacle of the voters being led by the nose into the Eisenhower camp by the Republican press majority, forgetting that a similar majority was flouted by the voters when Roosevelt was the candidate. They have been somewhat mollified by their 1960 victory. I am convinced that what "editorial influence" really amounts to is an impact of opinion and argument upon the reader that very rarely results in any shattering overturn of his established beliefs, but serves rather to give a verbal pattern to the pulls and biases and leanings and latent controls that are constantly exerted over him by his fixed mores and the interests of the family, social, industrial, intellectual, and religious groups with which he is affiliated. Thus Greeley was doing "all their thinking and theory" for Illinois farmers only in the sense that he was giving form to their beliefs. When one of them would ask another what he thought about the Clay Compromise, he would scratch his head, and say, "Wal, what does Horace say about it?" He really knew what basically he believed, but Horace was his spokesman. Most "editorial influence," I am convinced, is little more than the process of providing a statement that may be arranged conformably and comfortably with the reader's own deeply-rooted tenets of theory and behavior.

Does this sound cynical? I do not think it is. It would be disastrous if our people were so febrile and unstable as to be subject to a basic overturn of opinion every time an important issue came up. I am proud to be a "square" in a nation of "squares," and I am sure that even the "beatniks" are subject to more and stronger group controls than they themselves realize. Liberals and conservatives, young and old, are more or less bound by preconceptions and group ideologies; and a good newspaper editor does not set himself up as a professional iconoclast.

Of course, a crucial event, or series of events, or some important revelation, may change opinions on an important issue; and discussions of such events and developments are doubtless more important than the general run of partisan commentary and argument.

Certainly it is a newspaper's first and chief function to print the news, fairly and honestly, and to dig behind and beneath what Walter Lippmann once called the "overt news" for hidden facts and significances which are needed to fill out the complete picture of events and situations.

The newspaper has a second and very important function, to interpret the news with as little bias as is humanly possible. In these days of highly complex national and international economic, political, and social problems, such interpretation is a necessity for the presentation of an adequate picture of world events, movements, and ideas.

It is also the duty of a good newspaper to present varied opinion—the editorial-management opinion of the editorial column, the "columns" of facts and views by signed contributors, and the opinions of public figures in the news reports.

Now, if all of this, taken together, constitutes a process of "molding public opinion," then I agree that this is what newspapers do. At any rate, the performance of the functions I have just listed constitutes, in realistic terms, the impact of the modern press sometimes referred to as "influence" or "power."

One of the fallacies of which some contemporary observers are guilty is the notion that the newspaper (and indeed, the metropolitan newspaper alone) is the only communications medium by which the people are informed and their thinking guided. This leads certain writers to view the mergers and consolidation of such papers, which constitute a striking phenomenon of modern press history, as a trend toward monopoly of opinion. Thus Morris L. Ernst discusses the consolidation of metropolitan newspapers in one of his books under the heading, "The Vanishing Marketplace of Thought." But this marketplace is really very complex; it includes many factors and agencies of communication. Some are in print, as the daily newspapers, the weekly papers, the news magazines, periodicals in great variety, topical books, and so on. Some are electronic, as radio and television, which now give more time than ever before to news events and situations. Some are found in public speech, newsreels, records, group discussions, and many other means of getting news and ideas into circulation.

Neither thought nor its marketplace is going to vanish because of the increase of one-newspaper cities, or single-ownership cities. This tendency has been an inescapable feature of modern industrial development. I can say frankly that I should like to see more newspapers, with more individualistic editing; and I shall point out later some signs of a return to a freer competition. But we must all admit that today's list of so-called "monopoly" newspapers, in our largest single-paper cities and in cities with single ownership of a pair of papers, includes some of the best journalistic performances in the country. For example, the *Minneapolis Star*, the *Louisville Courier-Journal*, the *New Orleans Times-Picayune*, the *Kansas City Star*, and the *Des Moines Register* all rate positions among the leaders in American newspaper journalism.

Moreover, although I have spent so much time delving in the history of journalism that I have strong sympathies for many of the papers and the editors of the past, I must here declare my belief that we have today in America better newspapers than we have ever had before—more painstaking reporting, fuller coverage, better writing, fairer discussion, than in the days of Hearst and Pulitzer, Godkin and Dana, Greeley and Bennett, Ben Franklin and Isaiah Thomas.

I make this declaration of belief with the full knowledge that generalizations about newspapers are usually misleading. Such statements leave too much unsaid. For years I was accustomed to say to my classes (paraphrasing, I now think, a Voltairean epigram I had picked up somewhere) that the only safe generalization about newspapers is that no generalization about them is safe. There is a great variety in newspapers today, in spite of what critics say about their "deadly uniformity." Some of them are excellent by almost anyone's standards; but there are now, and always have been, some papers that are a disgrace to the profession, and some of these have large circulations.

Let me quote a paragraph from an address by a famous New York editor:

There are blackguards and blackmailers now in plenty, who by hook or crook get access to the columns even of respectable newspapers, but they are fewer in proportion than they ever were before. There is intemperate denunciation now—and mere personal abuse, and the fiercest partisan intolerance; the newspapers are crude; the newspapers are shallow; the newspapers are coarse, are unjust, are impertinent; they meddle in private affairs; they distort the news to suit their own views; they wield their tremendous power to feed fat private grudges; they are too often indebted, as Sheridan said of an antagonist, to their imaginations for their facts; they crave sensations that they may turn a few extra dirty pennies, and are reckless of truth, so they can print a story that will become the talk of the town. . . .

This indictment was uttered by Whitelaw Reid in 1872 in the course of an address delivered at the University of the City of New York just before he succeeded Horace Greeley as editor of the *New York Tribune*. My excerpt does not represent the tone of the entire address by any means, for Reid was too wise to allow his observations to fly away on the wings of wide generalizations. Always a scholar and always an advocate of the professional attitudes in journalism, he had at this time much to say also about the better newspapers and about contemporary progress in journalism. He recognized, as we all must, that progress never holds to a straight line, ascending, beautiful and uninterrupted, to the ideal plane. He knew that we cannot appreciate excellence in the newspaper field or anywhere else without recognizing concomitant faults and failures.

It is interesting to check the schedule of charges that Reid brought against the press of the early 1870's with those that may be levied against our newspapers ninety years later. Some of them are quite as valid today as they were then; some refer to abuses far less common now than in "the good old days." A study of the criticisms of the newspaper press from the time of its beginnings in the first decade of the seventeenth century to the present adds a tremendous amount to one's understanding of the history of the press itself and of popular ideas; this is a neglected field of investigation. And, of course, contemporary strictures should never be shrugged off but always carefully considered. Press criticism is a lively trade today, plied both inside and outside newspaper circles, on the one hand by those who understand contemporary publication problems, and on the other by many who are merely intoxicated by waters from utopian springs.

The press will always have need of lively—and informed—criticism. I have remarked that newspapers are much better today than they were a hundred, or fifty, or even twenty years ago. But that, after all, is not the important consideration. Are they good enough for the present? In these times of great peril, when the fate of western civilization seems to hang in the balance and the necessity for our people to know and understand world situations is paramount, are the newspapers good enough for today—and for the future? Never were the burdens of responsible journalism heavier.

The gravest fault of the newspaper press has long been the disproportionate space and emphasis given to merely exciting and entertaining content at the expense of what is significantly important. The Japanese used to refer to these two grand categories as "light" and "heavy" news and to set them apart in their papers. In the United States we have sometimes called them "soft" and "hard" news. Thoughtful journalists generally recognize the distinction. In an address at the University of Missouri in 1950, Arthur Hays Sulzberger said: "We have two choices. We can report, and define, and explain, in honest perspective, the great issues which are now before the nation and the world; or we can ignore or minimize these issues and divert our readers to less important, but no doubt more entertaining, matters. My vote goes for the paper that informs." Of course, there is always the danger that "hard" news may be hard to read, but good journalistic writing makes important news interesting. At the very least, a skillful writer takes the casual reader by the hand and leads him into the field of some important new development or set of facts or events and keeps him there for a while.

This "hard" news certainly should not be thought of only as reports of international affairs and stories of scientific developments—two much-discussed categories, both of which are important and both of which, by the way, have shown space increases in American newspapers in recent years. No, local news must always bulk large in most papers; and the news of government on all levels, of the schools, of the arts, and so on, must receive due attention.

I do not mean to raise my voice against entertainment in our newspapers, especially when it is on the plane of ordinary intelligence. A newspaper has to be readable and attractive or it will lose its audience. But there is a great range in entertainment: informative news and features may be absorbingly interesting to the average reader when presented with skill, and wit and humor in picture and text may leaven a loaf that seems too heavy. Yet the honest critic cannot condone filling a paper with stuff that is merely catchy and shocking. I find myself increasingly disturbed by the overplay of violence on our front pages and on television and motion-picture screens. Of course, there is too much actual violence in the world today, and there always has been too much; but has the time not come to reconsider the question of the deranged excitement of readers and viewers for profit and to take perhaps a more civilized view of the portrayal of the modern scene?

Prediction is a rash business at best; but if I am to be as candid as I set out to be in this little essay, I must now express my convictions about certain fundamental trends in the development of today's journalism. I therefore drape myself here in the mantle of the prophet and ascend his tripod and speak forth as boldly as I can. I do believe that in this era of entertainment by television, radio, cinema, and improved phonographic devices, the newspaper is being maneuvered more and more into the position of a recorder and expounder of events and situations and that it will in the future tend to abandon most of the old, bad, irresponsible patterns that characterized the period of "yellow journalism." The demoralizing and unprofitable competition of the "extras" has disappeared in the face of radio and television "flashes"; the noxious abuses of the "gutter journalism" of the "tabs" of the twenties have declined in most of our cities and tend to disappear in some; the place of the newspaper of the future as record and review for sober reading comes to be indicated more plainly month by month.

Indeed, there appears upon the horizon today what seems to be a revolution in newspaper journalism. It comes from four sources. First, new technologies in phototypesetting, "cold type," plastic plates, and offset printing (none of them fully developed today but certain to be greatly extended on economical levels in the future) will lower the costs of printing plants and their operation and eventually increase the number of newspapers serving the public. Second, the great contemporary shifts in population to exurban communities, to suburbs, and to line settlements are joining in this stimulus to the founding of new papers; most of these begin as "throw-aways," then change to pay-weeklies, and many eventually become dailies. Third, we see some metropolitan dailies abandoning their roles as merely city and regional papers to seek, by means of various new technologies, truly national circulations—something that the wide expanse of the United States has hitherto seemed to preclude. Fourth, as I have already pointed out, the competition of the electronic and other media tends to force newspaper content into a somewhat different pattern than that of the past sixty-five years. If all of these movements taken together do not seem to warrant the application of the word "revolution" to the newspaper journalism of the 1960's, I should be content to adopt a more modest term and call it "radical change." But that sensational innovations in the business and profession of making newspapers are facing us in the immediate future seems beyond question.

I realize that I have oversimplified my description of these shifts and changes; I can only suggest here that newspapers confront many complex problems and dangers in making the major transitions demanded by the new world of communication.

I wish to close this commentary, which I have entitled a "testament," with a statement of personal ideals about journalism. I think these beliefs form a kind of "religio journalistici," and I shall set them forth as three related principles.

First, however, I must reconcile my idealism with my full acceptance of the fact that journalism *is* a business as well as a profession, and—to put it baldly—that a newspaper must make some profit in order to survive. I concur heartily in the first declaration of Walter Williams' Journalist's Creed, "I believe in the profession of journalism"; but I recognize that every profession in the modern world is in part a business. Doctors, lawyers, clergymen, even teachers, are paid, and sometimes very well paid, for their professional services. So must the journalist be, and that means, of course, that his newspaper must be at least a going concern. On the other hand, it is wrong to put profits above fitting and proper service. A good friend of mine, the editor of a great newspaper, recently said: "The first function of a newspaper is to stay alive." No, that is not the first function: a paper that does not perform its proper service does not deserve to stay alive. My friend was betrayed by an epigram. He will agree with me in theory, as he does in practice, that every great newspaper strives with utmost effort to fuse and blend a high quality of service with a reasonable profit.

For the first of the three principles of our confession of faith we find a text ready to our use in the Old Testament Scriptures, where, in that most extraordinary of narratives whose sweeping strokes tell the Hebrew story of the Creation, we are told: "And God said, Let there be light: and there was light." Here is the summation of the whole duty of the journalist. There is a tradition that the first words ever printed were *Fiat Lux;* and it must indeed be true that when Johan Gutenberg laid the first type-form for his great Bible on the bed of his primitive press some five hundred years ago, those words were included. Here we have a great symbol, for *Fiat Lux* is the motto of all printing, as it is of journalism, and indeed of all general communication. If the ideal indicated by these words had not been cherished with no less than religious fervor by successive generations of journalists, the activities of all men of power would still be veiled in secrecy, and the people would walk in darkness as far as the understanding of great events and situations is concerned.

The second principle for which the journalist has an innate and instinctive devotion is that of democracy. In any mass communication effort, it is *demos* that is aimed at; the printing press, as we have been reminded by many writers, has always been the great tool of popular movements, the engine of democracy. Your real journalist, whether or not he ever talks about it, has an inherent feeling for the popular audience; he likes people as people.

And of course the third and final principle of our creed is devotion to truth—which, in this case, means simply honesty in dealing with facts. There is no need to be pretentious about it, but the plainest reality is that the reporter has to be true to the facts, true to himself, and true to his readers, if he is to work within the framework of self-respect and good professional behavior. I am all too well acquainted with the pseudo-cynicism that some newspapermen wear as a kind of cloak for protection against criticism and pressures. But beneath all that, they have an extraordinary loyalty to truth as an ideal.

The economist John Maynard Keynes once remarked that there are "two branches of religion—high and low, mystical sleep-walkers and practical idealists." Doubtless there are many (the great Quaker Rufus Jones comes to mind) who have combined the "high" and the "low." I have to confess that throughout my later life I have been little concerned with *Dieu-en-Ciel*, to use the term by which Sartre makes this same distinction, though I have no inclination to quarrel with my friends who accept mystical attitudes with comfortable faith. But I do find, in my own naïve way, the idea of God on Earth supremely important, as it is exemplified by sincere and zealous devotion to what thinking and working men conceive to be the highest aims and the best things in this our life. If this is "low" religion, it is still good enough to inspire our best efforts toward high objectives and our faith in the attainment of such ideals. And so I do not hesitate to speak of the three principles I have enunciated as forming the creed of the working "religion of the journalist."

15

Time Enough

I HAVE HAD A FULL LIFE. I have always felt that it must be not only full but well ordered to be worth living. As a boy in high school, I experimented for a time in scheduling my week in fifteen-minute periods. These timetables I often flouted; but they were a guide to the employment of my time, and they were an interesting plaything. I had derived the idea, which fascinated me, from Benjamin Franklin's tabular design for perfectionism in the *Autobiography*. When I was in college, I tried such calendars again for a few months, finding that the class and recreation schedules already imposed upon me lent themselves to that kind of bookkeeping.

I have never spent much time in playing games; but as a college lad I was surprised to learn, when I totted up my figures for the week, how many quarter-hours I was giving to "conversation." No small part of this category was devoted, I am sure, to bull sessions. I soon gave up my foolish timetables, though I believe the thought of them continued to influence my life for a long time.

Probably many of the college hours that I classified as devoted to "activities" were wasted. At least, I came to think so; and one of the reasons that I left Simpson College at the end of my third year and took my senior work at the University of Chicago was that I felt that my time schedules had got out of hand. At Simpson I had found myself participating in so many interesting enterprises that I gave only a minimum of my attention to such esoteric matters as courses of study; at Chicago I was an outsider who had appeared after friendships had been made and cliques formed, and besides I was rather submerged in a larger student body. So there I did give most of my time to my studies. I attended an occasional show at a downtown theater and became a George M. Cohan fan. But I entered only one "outside activity" at the University—the oratorical contest. This I won; and later I represented Chicago at the meet of the Northern Oratorical League, held that year at the University of Wisconsin, and felt no little satisfaction in gaining second place. But I did not have time enough that year for much besides study and my oratorical effort.

As soon as I had my degree, I plunged into newspaper work in the county-seat town of Marengo, Iowa. I have heard men working on metropolitan dailies talk wistfully of their hope sometime to own a country weekly, where life would be a lazy, bucolic existence; but experience has taught me that all kinds of newspaper work are full of stress and strain. About all that one can claim for ease on a weekly is that there are two or three days of the seven that may sometimes be less harried than the others, and that deadlines are not quite as arbitrary as they are on the dailies. But there is a less definite division of labor on the weekly, so that the editor must now and then turn his hand to almost any task in the office; and he sometimes finds himself, in doing one job, trying to outrace himself doing another.

The profession and business of journalism, to which most of my life has been dedicated, suffers more than most occupations under the tyranny of the clock. This is especially true of the daily. The clock ticks out the deadlines by which the daily paper is conducted. There is a deadline for the reporter, a deadline for the copy desk, a deadline for make-up, a deadline for the presses. Then for each edition the series is repeated throughout the day, and so for each day of the year, and for every year of a newspaperman's life.

For some this means hurry and scurry and rush, and hypertension and ulcers and high blood pressure; but what it means to the better journalist is orderly planning and steady, concentrated work. It is a major fault for a newspaper worker to be slow by habit, but it is a fault that I have never seen corrected by fuss and flurry. If my memory of Trollope serves me, there is (or was) an English country saying, "It's dogged as does it." Unremitting perseverance is the important thing, and deadlines are made more easily by good planning and even-drive than by the hubbub of hurry.

The journalist has named the cumulative instant, to which his timetable builds, a "deadline" because everything that comes after it is dead for that edition, thus dramatizing in a word the perishability of news. This fact is part of his business, and he has to accept it. But I am profoundly convinced that the recurrent emphasis on points of time that have no real significance has a tendency to distort his concept of time in general and what it means and is. And this conviction extends beyond newspaper work to include all hectic and overstrained employment, be it plane transporation, television production, advertising, or indeed urban life in general. Christopher Morley once wrote an "Epitaph for Any New Yorker":

> I, who all my life had hurried,
> > Came to Peter's crowded gate;
> And, as usual, was worried,
> > Fearing that I might be late.
> So, when I began to jostle
> > (I forgot that I was dead)
> Patient smiled the old Apostle:
> > "Take your eternity," he said.[*]

But let me resume my narrative of one man's wrestling with Father Time. During my country newspaper years, I occasionally found a pliant hour, at night or on Sundays, to do some writing for magazines, with just enough success to whet my appetite for authorship. I have told something about this in another essay in this book, and also how I wrote for my own paper some pieces on literary subjects that I printed mainly to satisfy my own deeply-felt need for self-expression. There was one series that I called "Literary Enthusiasms" and a later one entitled "Six Prophets Out of the Middle West." These won some praise over the state and from those to whom I sent marked copies; and I decided that the schedule of my hours and days was, after all, maladjusted to what I wished most to do. So I sold my paper and entered Columbia University as a candidate for the doctor of philosophy degree, which I supposed was necessary to qualify me for the college teaching field. In the new life to which I then looked forward I expected to find ample time for the writing I wished so much to do.

But when I became a college teacher, I found that grading papers, advising students, and attending committee meetings, in addition to the always stimulating and enjoyable exercise of meeting classes, left little time for

[*] From *Parsons Pleasure* by Christopher Morley. Copyright 1923-1950 by Christopher Morley. Published by J. B. Lippincott Company.

a would-be writer. It was then that I developed my philosophy of Time Enough—which is simply the principle that anyone has time enough for anything he really wants to do. Anything within reason, of course, and under ordinary circumstances. One must make one's choices. Anything a person wants to do, if he wants hard enough to do it and if it is within his powers, he will find time for.

He finds time for it through his allocation of his "extra time"—which is the time left over from the duties that his regular employment demands. The shortened work week automatically furnishes, in our modern life, most of these hours of exemption from prescribed tasks. But orderly and efficient workers who know how to plan, and whose terms of employment do not include actual punching of time clocks, can make themselves still more of this "extra time"; they will earn it by their superior organization and their mastery of smooth-running operation. And then, let us hope that in these precious hours they have made for themselves they may find their heart's desire—they may do what they want most to do. . . . Yet it would not be realistic to forget that somehow or sometime our fine plans may be cut short and we may be forced to yield to an ultimate determinant and say, each of us: "Yes, this is my allotment—but this too is Time Enough."

We have a wide range of choices as to how to spend our "extra time." Sleep is a bidder for a sizable portion of it. Television is a greedy newcomer. Social life nearly always lays claim to a great share. Games often take many hours—playing card games, watching athletic contests, even solving crossword puzzles. Work, to supplement and improve regular employment; recreations and sports, such as golf and tennis, for fun and for physical benefit; reading, for pleasure or profit or both—the list is a long one. A person may dabble a bit in many fields, but he cannot give much time to any one without sacrificing others. When a man tells me, "But I don't have time to read books!" I know he means, "I don't care to allocate any of my 'extra time' to reading books." He has time enough to do anything he wishes very much to do. Anything within reason, under ordinary circumstances.

And thus I made my professional timetable so that I should have time enough for research, study, and writing. This meant giving up many things on my own part and indulgence on the part of others. It meant some reductions in recreations and in social life, and it meant help from an understanding wife and a co-operative daughter. It meant spending most evenings until midnight and later, as well as many Sundays and holidays, working in my study. All this may sound like the story of an austere life of self-sacrifice—like that of a medieval monk-scholar. But as a matter of fact, it was far from that; it really integrated the various things I wished most to do. It included many pleasures of family life, happy hours in the garden, an occasional sudden picnic in the woods, and so on. I had time enough to do a job, live a life, and complete the circle with the writing and research that meant so much to me.

But a new phase of my adventures with time began when I was persuaded to undertake administrative duties. Then my office cares developed a tendency to follow me into my home and study—a vicious pattern that I had to struggle against more consciously when I moved from Iowa to Missouri. Came the great GI invasion from 1946 to 1950, when the veterans of the Second World War descended upon our campus, as I have told in another place. These were good students, stimulating and earnest, anxious to make up for lost time, but they knocked our professorial timetables galley-west. . . . And this entire episode put me to thinking further about time and its meaning.

The visit of a group of Latin-American editors to the School of Journalism added something to my ideas on the subject. The group was to be with us only two days, and I made a careful schedule for them, which they cheerfully disregarded. They were fifty minutes late finishing breakfast the first morning; they became progressively later at each of their day's appointments; in spite of readjustments, they managed to make the president of the University wait half an hour on them. They capped the climax at the end of the second day when they kept an audience at the University Club (which then made a rule of always beginning and ending its programs on the dot) a full hour before appearing to offer what proved to be a brilliant series of short addresses. Sometime during the two-days' visit, I remonstrated a little with a visitor from Chile.

"Have you ever visited Spain?" he asked me.

"No," I said.

"A great country, but a little one, you would say. A poor country, but a rich one in many things. It is *turbando*—what you call "upsetting," is it not? You would be upset by their lack of care about time, I think. They have a saying there that because there is never any hurry in Spain, nobody is ever late to a meeting, because nobody is ever on time!"

I suppose that hurry is the devil-mother of many— perhaps most—of the diseases that beset us in this our modern life.

I noticed the way my small grandchildren treated

time. Did you ever see a child *hurry*, of his own voli-
tion? He may move fast in a game, but he has no con-
ception of *hurry*. In his infantile wisdom, he knows that
he has "all the time in the world." Watches are only
pretty toys to him. His sole awareness of time is that
which is forced upon him by his mother's call to come in
from play or to go to bed—each a summons that seems
to him quite unreasonable. I think that one of the chief
differences between childhood and adulthood is that
which stems from the little child's complete obliviousness
to time measurement. . . . Time, however, marches on.
School brings some knowledge of time's tyranny, which
grows with every year and every new responsibility.

Yet once in a while the grownup slips back into a
blessed infancy undisturbed by clocks. Years ago, on a
holiday, I lost my watch and was the happier for two
weeks without it. E. B. White once told about a youth-
ful excursion when he and another boy started out in a
Model "T" Ford, with the wide road before them and
both of them "full of the time of day." The youngsters,
it is clear, were comparatively heedless of time as a
continuum, but greatly concerned with time as experience.

This seems to me an extremely important distinction.
I believe that we must try to give each of these concepts
its full recognition and its proper place. Our lives are a
continual compromise between them.

In everyday routine, time is mainly a continuum for
us, so that we get into the habit of thinking of it solely as
measured by the clock and the calendar. Each minute is
composed of an equal number of ticked-off seconds,
each hour is struck at equal intervals, and each day has
exactly twenty-four hours—never twenty-three or twenty-
five, but twenty-four forever and ever, world without end.

For the longer units we turn from clock to calendar; and we find that, though months are annoyingly unequal, they are made up into equal years, except for one strayed day that luckily finds a place in February waiting for it once in each quadrennium. The pattern for these regular notches on the scale that go on through centuries and milleniums of time is provided, we are told, by the movements of our own planet in relation to those of other heavenly bodies.

But when astronomers talk about time in their terms, when certain philosophers insist that there is no such thing as time because we always live in the eternal Now, when poet-historian Carlyle writes repeatedly that the only fragment of time we know is merely a bridge between two eternities, when theologians declare that time is but a prelude to eternal glory or eternal pain—then we get the swing of the constellations all mixed up with the glitter of the heavenly streets and the flames of hell and we fall back easily upon the reliable ticking of the clock, which has formed a steady continuum throughout the ages (or at least since Pope Silvester II contrived the first one in 996 A.D.) in order to settle our minds.

Yet it is obvious that the clock and calendar give us merely the pattern, and that there is a second dimension of time that affords more meaning. There is a vast difference to me in the comparative values of the hours of my life. About a third of them I spend in sleep, some in thankless routine jobs, many in satisfying tasks; but there are some moments, hours, days, even weeks that have pleasure, agony, or meaning for me that no technique of measurement can compass. As I think back over my life, I recall many such experiences. Some of them I have chronicled in this book; others have seemed too intimate—our early married life at Rose Cottage in Marengo, an unforgettable holiday at "Tapiola" in the Long's Peak region of Colorado, certain sharp disappointments I should like to forget and certainly shall not detail here, a few great personal shocks that seemed almost to stop the flow of my life. And there are the abiding joys of many friendships—more than I can ever deserve. From my childhood I recall some lines of that once popular but now forgotten dramatic poem, Bailey's *Festus*:

> We live in deeds, not years; in thoughts, not breaths;
> In feelings, not in figures on a dial.
> We should count time by heart-throbs. . . .

I shall always treasure some remembrances of moments of acute perception of beauty—an unexpected sight of Fujiyama in the early morning light, a vision of the Grand Tetons breaking through the mist, a glimpse of *l'éclair vert* just as the top rim of the setting sun sank into the Bay of Biscay on a calm evening. Such moments still retain a luminescence in memory that mark them as possessing values far beyond those of what we call everyday living.

Let me relate one such incident. When I was a boy, my father used to send me out into the country to do farm work through most of the summer months. He thought that it was good for a town boy to get "hardened up" by pitching hay and shocking grain, and also that his son, who was to follow in his own footsteps as a country editor, ought to learn something about agricultural operations. He was right on both counts, of course, though it was an ordeal for me, especially during the first two weeks, when sore muscles cried out with every exertion and sweat-caked overalls were hard to get into at dawn. But one hot July afternoon on that farm something happened to me that I have never forgotten and never shall forget. A storm had come up at about four o'clock, and we were hurrying a last load of hay in from the field to get it mowed away before the tempest broke. The air was filled with the suspense before a storm, we shouted to the excited team drawing the wagon, our spirits were caught up in a kind of contest with the elements; and then I looked up at the advancing storm cloud. It came out of the northwest, and it was of that tragic, slate-purple color that denotes impending hail. And, then, cutting up into the midst of this great cloud of even color was the long, sun-bathed, smooth bend of a hill covered with newly shocked oats; and this entire hill-curve, bearing its little tepees of oat-shocks, was a very light, bright gold against the purple sky. I suppose I saw this grand and beautiful sight for as much as three minutes as we rushed along that rough pasture trail to the farmyard, but I have remembered it vividly ever since and recalled it often. It is difficult to compare aesthetic values with others, but I think that those three minutes meant more to me than many other three-week periods in my life—perhaps more than some three-month stretches.

Such moments that produce memorable effects upon us—and even sharp breaks in the flow of our lives—are analagous to crises in history that interrupt the often meaningless succession of dynasties and administrations. Thus certain tremendous events—the storming of the Bastille, the bomb dropped on Hiroshima—carry far more significance than the whole of such a period as the tenth century A.D. Such phenomena light up whole eras; and suddenly history is no longer mere chronology, but a succession of events that men must evaluate. In modern times, these illuminating episodes seem more frequent than in past ages—an effect that is partly due, of course, to our own perspective. Yet world-shaking events do shake more often a world with the tighter organization of today. Or it may be that an increasing freedom from the traditions that once tended to keep mankind in a strait and narrow way detract increasingly from the concept of time as mere continuum. Gertrude Stein makes a good observation in her biography of Picasso: "The Twentieth Century is a time when everything cracks . . . everything isolates itself; it is a more splendid thing than a period when everything follows itself." Such times, I submit, come also in the lives of individuals, and they also are splendid.

This richer, goodlier chronology that is formed by a succession of great events is the one that engages the attention of philosophers, poets, and novelists. There is a passage in Ernest Hemingway's *Green Hills of Africa* in which he wrote hopefully of "a fourth and fifth dimension" in the art of writing. He was vague in regard to the matter, and I do not wish to confuse the issue further than the critics have already obscured it, but it seems probable to me that Hemingway had in mind the three dimensions of any physical scene (with emphasis on depth), and that he then added time as a continuum for a fourth dimension, and then, to cap it all, time as experience for a fifth. If a scene be so regarded by a novelist, he must find the fifth dimension richer than all the others in the same proportion that the human spirit is more important than its background.

What I have been trying to say is something that philosophers have been pointing out ever since the time of Zeno. It is really something very obvious: time has meaning according to the experience with which we fill it. Of course, the alarm clock will ring tomorrow morning, and I shall answer its summons, and most readers of this page will be answering similar strident and hateful sounds; and we shall all fulfill our engagements more or less on the minute. That is the way the workaday world must be run. But there are means of humanizing odious schedules by building into them incidents of meaning, variety, and stimulation.

A few years ago I wearied of the breakfast-newspaper routine. I had no thought of giving up the reading of my morning paper, but I resented having the latest sex-murder and the newest turmoil in Washington spoil the flavor of my grapefruit and turn my oatmeal sour in my mouth. Besides, it seemed wrong to me to start the day in a mood of indignant frustration induced by a review of what was wrong in the world. About this time, my friend Sherman Baker, of the Thomas Y. Crowell publishing house, dropped by and left me a copy of a new book edited by J. Donald Adams and published by Crowell under the title *Treasure Chest;* it was composed of short selections from classics and near-classics, some of which Adams had used on his page in the *New York Times Book Review.* I liked the anthology and proposed to my wife that we postpone the reading of the morning news and that we read aloud at breakfast every day one of the Adams selections—from the Book of Job, Plato's dialogues, the letters of Cicero, essays by Montaigne or Thoreau, a Steinbeck novel, or something else from a rich table of contents. But would this not make me late getting away to the office or to a class? It would, indeed; and I had no wish to emulate the dizzy dash of a Dagwood for his morning bus. So why not set the alarm fifteen minutes earlier? That we did, and thereafter breakfasts were something to look forward to with anticipation and look backward upon with pleasure—as well as a good springboard for the day. So I sat down and wrote Baker a little note of appreciation, telling him of our family plan. He evidently put my letter into the hands of a publicity man, because soon a number of little items appeared in literary columns about Mott's morning readings. But the editor of the book page of the *Chicago Tribune* seemed to me to miss the point when she commented that this was all very well for an academic retreat, but it would never fit with the rush and hurry of a city worker's morning. Alas, it would not fit with rush and hurry anywhere. It fitted with our time-continuum only because we were willing to displace fifteen minutes' morning snooze by a similar space of stimulating thought. It fitted less with Dagwood's dash than with the free man's declaration, "I have time enough to do what I want to do."

Not a completely free man, of course, but a man free from the bondages of rush and mere conformity. What I wish to assert with some insistence, on this the last page of my book, is that, although we are all a part of the clock-and-calendar system on which the world must be run, although we are bound to that rack for life, we ought boldly to accept the second dimension of time, so that we shall occasionally stand up and say, each for himself, "I have time enough—enough and to spare for what I really wish most to do."

No matter how burdened or harried we are, there is always time for what we want most if we make it. There is time enough in a week for that week; there is time enough in a year for what we want to make of that year.

There is time enough in a life.